TONGUES: FROM CONFUSION TO UNDERSTANDING

*Understanding the Ministry
of the Holy Spirit and Prayer*

by
James A. McMenis

Tongues: From Confusion to Understanding
Understanding the Ministry of the Holy Spirit and Prayer
by James A. McMenis

Printed in the United States of America

ISBN 9781615795765

www.xulonpress.com

CONTENTS

SPECIAL THANKS!

To my wife, Chrissy, for all you do every day that enables me to be the best I can be. I wouldn't be where I am without you. When God gave you to me, He gave me beyond all that I could have asked or envisioned. As a wife and mother, you are constantly amazing me. I love you and thank Him for you!

To my mom, Lola McMenis (1937-2008) and to my dad, Jessup "Al" McMenis (1930-1999), for never doubting my calling to preach the Gospel and for the undying love and support you have given me. I will be eternally grateful!

To the Members and Partners of Word of God Ministries, your support and encouragement fuels my passion for the ministry of His Word. I love you and thank God for you!

To all who assisted me in the writing of this book, Naomi Lawler and Keiah Ellis, thanks for all of your assistance. I couldn't have done it without you. You and your families are assets to the ministry and the Body of Christ. I love and appreciate you!

Chapter 1

IS SPEAKING IN TONGUES THE EVIDENCE OF THE BAPTISM OF THE HOLY GHOST?

The Invitation

"Have you received the baptism of the Holy Ghost with the evidence of speaking in tongues?"

This has become a familiar question at invitation time in many denominational and non-denominational churches. There are even churches that include in their statement of beliefs that, "We believe in the baptism of the Holy Ghost with the evidence of speaking in tongues." Every week, young and old alike are offered this invitation; and many accept but then leave the service still confused, not understanding the mysterious, unintelligible language that they have been strongly encouraged to speak. Often, preachers and church leaders will spend hours praying with and laying hands on someone, waiting for any indistinguishable sounds to fall from his or her lips. Finally, after several repetitive utterances are made by the believer, celebration begins for this one who has *supposedly* received the Holy Spirit with evidence of speaking an indiscernible language known as 'tongues'. But is speaking in tongues the only evidence of the baptism of the Holy Ghost? Despite the popular belief that it is, Scripture does not draw this conclusion. But sadly, for many, this teaching and practice has become as much doctrine as the death, burial and resurrection of Jesus!

As popular as this teaching is throughout church assemblies everywhere, there are many that are confused, and seek the truth on this highly debated issue. To truly begin the journey in understanding this topic, we must first recognize what is *speaking in tongues*. In order to do that we must understand the purpose of tongues – why it was introduced and what purpose does it accomplish. In this book, we are going to, without bias, look into the Word of God and find clear understanding of this topic, and finally answer the question "Is speaking in tongues the evidence of the baptism of the Holy Ghost?" based on scriptural proof from the Word of God. We need to know the truth!

What Are Tongues?

In the Old Testament, there is mention of ecstatic utterances that were spoken by wizards and those under the influence of familiar spirits, and there are also various chants and mantras spoken by believers and non-believers today. We will study these topics in a later chapter. For this portion of study, we will focus on the use of 'tongues' in the New Testament.

The use of the word 'tongues' in the New Testament can be translated into its original Greek language with one of three words: **Glossa**, which refers both to language and to the organ of the mouth, **Dialektos**, which means dialect or language, or **Heteroglossos,** which means foreigner, one of another language. The word 'tongue' occurs fifty times in the New Testament. One time it is specifically defined as "**cloven tongues like as of fire**" (Acts 2:3). Sixteen times it refers to the literal organ of the human mouth. Thirty-three times it refers to the known languages of the world. The word 'tongue' is never defined as the use of an ecstatic language that can not be understood, nor is this definition implied.

In Matthew 28, Jesus instructed his disciples to go forth and to teach all nations (v.19). But, the question then became, how could these disciples go forth and preach to all nations while limited to speaking and understanding only one or two languages? Well aware of their natural limitations, Jesus promised to give His disciples a miraculous, supernatural ability to speak foreign languages they had not previously spoken, studied or learned, for the purpose of spreading the Gospel to all nations or dialects, in order to carry out His commission. This sign was promised in Mark 16:17, when Jesus said they would "**speak with new tongues.**" Calling this ability a "sign" indicates to us that this manifestation would not come through practice or natural means, but by instant power of the Holy Ghost. There are ten accounts in the Book of Acts where one or many received the gift of the Holy Ghost in His fullness, and only in two occasions other than Pentecost do we hear of speaking in tongues (other languages or dialects). These ten accounts are as follows: Acts 2:38, 4:8, 4:31, 6:5, 8:15, 9:17, 10:44, 11:24, 13:52, and 19:6. The two occasions, following the day of Pentecost, where the one who received the Holy Ghost also spoke in tongues are found in Acts 10:45-46 and 19:1-6. By further study of these occasions, we should be able to clearly understand this often misunderstood gift.

They Spoke with Other Tongues

"And they were filled with the Holy Ghost, and began to speak with other tongues, as the Spirit gave them utterance."
—ACTS 2:4

The word 'tongues' here in verse four is the Greek word *glossa*, which means a known language. But we don't need to be scholars in the Greek language to see that the words spoken at Pentecost through the gift of tongues were known languages of the world, and were understood by at least sixteen different regions and dialects, if we simply continue reading:

Now when this was noised abroad, the multitude came together, and were confounded, because that every many heard them speak in his own language.

> **And they were all amazed and marveled, saying one to another, Behold, are not all these which speak Galileans?**
>
> **And how hear we every man in our own tongue, wherein we were born?**
>
> **Parthians, and Medes, and Elamites, and the dwellers of Mesopotamia, and in Judaea, and Cappadocia, in Pontus, and Asia,**
>
> **Phrygia, and Pamphylia, in Egypt, and in the parts of Libya about Cyrene, and strangers of Rome, Jews and proselytes,**
>
> **Cretes and Arabians, we do hear them speak in our tongues the wonderful works of God.**
>
> — ACTS 2:6-11

It has been suggested that the gift of tongues is a "heavenly language," understood only by God or those gifted with interpretation. But the Bible is clear that, on the Day of Pentecost, both the disciples *and* those listening understood what was being spoken. All of the represented nations that were present heard the disciples speak in their own **"tongues the wonderful works of God"** (v. 11). God used the gift of tongues to get the gospel of the death, burial and resurrection of Jesus to everyone assembled there that day. Make no mistake about it—Jesus was preached!

In Acts 2:22-40, Peter preaches the message of Jesus as Lord and Christ, the Anointed One. In verse 32, he declared, **"This Jesus hath God raised up, whereof we are witnesses,"** in accordance to what Jesus said about our being His witnesses in Acts 1:8: **"But ye shall receive power, after that the Holy Ghost is come upon you: and ye shall be witnesses unto me both in Jerusalem, and in all Judaea, and in Samaria, and unto the uttermost part of the earth."**

The Holy Ghost came upon Peter that he might be a witness of Jesus. At the end of Peter's message, those present asked, "what shall we do?" And Peter said unto them, **"Repent, and be baptized every one of you in the name of Jesus Christ for the remission**

of sins, and ye shall receive the gift of the Holy Ghost" (Acts 2:37-38).

So while it is true that the gift of tongues was in operation on the Day of Pentecost, no one walked away that day lacking understanding. On the contrary, those of other dialects walked away with a clear understanding of God's saving grace offered through the gift of His Son Jesus, the Anointed One! The end result of the Pentecostal experience was that people got saved! **"Then they that gladly received his word were baptized: and that same day there were added unto them about three thousand souls"** (Acts 2:41). And that salvation resulted in those of other tongues or dialects returning to their homeland and telling the story of Jesus! And this is true of every ministry and spiritual gift. It will always lead the hearer to the work of redemption, every time.

The Evidence of the Baptism of the Holy Ghost

Isaiah prophesied,

Whom shall he teach knowledge? And whom shall he make to understand doctrine? Them that are weaned from the milk, and drawn from the breasts.

For precept must be upon precept; precept upon precept; line upon line, line upon line, here a little and there a little:

For with stammering lips and another tongue will he speak to this people.

To whom he said, This is the rest wherewith ye may cause the weary to rest; and this is the refreshing: yet they would not hear.

—ISAIAH 28:9-12

God said, through the prophet Isaiah, that He would teach His people (the Jews), but they would not hear. As a sign of the refreshing (the gift of His Spirit), He would cause men of other tongues (Gentiles) to speak to His people (Jews) and that they still would not listen. The Jews rejected the Messiah, Jesus the Anointed One, and as a sign of His coming, God said that He would use men of other tongues to preach to His people. Paul expounded on this in his letter to the Corinthians:

In the law it is written, With men of other tongues and other lips will I speak unto this people; and yet for all that will they not hear me, saith the Lord.

Wherefore, tongues are for a sign, not to them that believe, but to them that believe not: but prophesying serveth not for them that believe not, but for them which believe.

— 1 CORINTHIANS 14:21-22

God used the native tongue of the Gentiles as a sign to the Jews—the Messiah has come! The Gentiles (lost nations) had no knowledge of the Messiah or the gift of the Spirit. They were ignorant of the Word of God, the Law and the Prophets. The Jews had been taught and were not ignorant to God's promise. When a knowledgeable Jew would hear a foreigner to God's law witness Christ or the Messiah to him, it was a sign of the gift of the Spirit. How else could one of another tongue know of what had previously only been given to the Jews?

In both occasions where the Holy Ghost baptism was accompanied by speaking in tongues, it was Gentiles speaking in the presence of Jews! In Acts 10, Peter preached the circumcision (v.45) to the house of Cornelius, a Gentile (v. 22), in the company of Jews. When they heard the word, the Holy Ghost fell on them that heard (v. 44). In verse 45, God fulfills again what He spoke in Isaiah 28:11 – the Jews witnessed men of other tongues magnify God.

And they of the circumcision which believed were astonished, as many as came with Peter, because that on the Gentiles also was poured out the gift of the Holy Ghost. For they heard them speak with tongues, and magnify God.

— ACTS 10:45

In Acts 11, Peter returns to Jerusalem to inform the Apostles that the Gentiles had received the Word of God (v. 1). When Peter explained all that had transpired, the Jews contended with him. **"But Peter rehearsed the matter from the beginning, and expounded it by order unto them"** (v.4). From verse 4 through verse 18, Peter explained the sequence of events in order. Notice carefully what Peter said about Cornelius, and his household receiving salvation and the gift of the Holy Ghost. **"And as I began to speak, the Holy Ghost fell on them, as on us at the beginning."** Peter explained that Cornelius and his family received the same gift of tongues in the same way the disciples did on the day of Pentecost. Peter didn't coach Cornelius as some of us may have witnessed in some churches. He never informed him to speak meaningless utterances in a fast, repetitive manner until he "got the gift". This was an instantaneous, supernatural manifestation, equivalent to what happened on Pentecost. And in agreement with prophecy, it happened to Gentiles in the presence of Jews!

In Acts 19, the same objective was accomplished. In verse 10, we see that both Jews and Greeks heard the word of the Lord Jesus. We will study this occasion in greater detail a little later, where we will find that the third and final recorded manifestation of tongues is like the first two.

The Bible makes clear the evidence of the filling of the Holy Ghost. Whether the gift of tongues was used or not, one thing always remained the same in each situation: the Word of God was preached with boldness, power and authority.

And when they had prayed, the place was shaken where they were assembled together; and they were all filled with the Holy Ghost, and they spoke the Word of God with boldness.

— ACTS 4:31

Let's take a look at a few occasions where the filling of the Holy Ghost was manifested and the result (or evidence) was the Word of God was spoken with boldness, yet there is no mention of tongues. In Acts 8:14-17, Peter and John prayed and laid hands on the Samaritan believers, and the Bible says that they received the Holy Ghost, but there is no account of anyone speaking in tongues. In Acts 6:5-10, the Bible says that Stephen was a man full of faith and the Holy Ghost, but makes no mention of him speaking in tongues. But the Scripture does say that **"the word of God increased"** (v. 7). **"And they were not able to resist the wisdom and the spirit by which he spake"** (v. 10). The Bible, once again, declares that the Word of God, which *is* the wisdom of God, was the evidence of being filled with the Holy Ghost. **"The Spirit of the LORD spake by me, and his <u>word</u> was in my tongue"** (2 Samuel 23:2, emphasis mine). This verse declares that when the Spirit speaks it is the Word of God that comes forth. The Holy Ghost and the Word of God are in perfect agreement.

> **For there are three that bear record in heaven, the Father, the Word, and the Holy Ghost: and these three are one.**
> — 1 JOHN 5:7

The Word of God has always been the manifestation of the Spirit on man's tongue. Jesus said, **"The Spirit of the Lord is upon me, because he hath anointed me to preach the gospel..."** (Luke 4:18). God, His Word, and His Spirit never change. In Malachi 3:6, God says **"I change not"** and in James 1:17, the Bible says that with God there is **"no variableness, neither shadow of turning."** With that in mind, notice the following verse of Scripture:

> **The Lord hath given me the tongue of the learned, that I should know how to speak a word in season to him that is weary: he wakeneth morning by morning, he wakeneth mine ear to hear as the learned.**
> — ISAIAH 50:4

This Scripture declares that God gives us the tongue and ear of the learned that we might hear and speak His Word to him that is weary. This is exactly what happened in the Book of Acts. In Acts 4:8, the Bible says that Peter was **"filled with the Holy Ghost"** as he ministered the word by which five thousand became believers

(v. 4). Notice what was said of Peter and John following this great outpouring: "**Now when they saw the boldness of Peter and John, and perceived that they were unlearned and ignorant men, they marveled; and they took knowledge of them, that they had been with Jesus**" (v. 13). They didn't marvel at some indiscernible language that they spoke, but they marveled at the boldness in which they spoke the Word of God – boldness that made the lame man to walk again.

One would be hard pressed to find one case in the entire canon of Scripture where someone was healed because of some ecstatic unknown prayer language. It's not possible because there are no accounts of such an event; however, what we *do* find, time and time again, is that the Word of God spoken by a man full of the Holy Ghost wrought miracles, healing, salvation and deliverance.

The Word of God has been written by the power of the Holy Ghost. "**For the prophecy came not in old time by the will of man: but holy men of God spake as they were moved by the Holy Ghost**" (2 Peter 1:21).

The Bible says in Matthew 18:16 and Deuteronomy 19:15 that in the mouth of two or three witnesses every word is established. I pray that, by the Word of God, we have established that the scriptural evidence of the fullness or baptism of the Holy Ghost is boldness in speaking the Word of God!

Chapter 2

CAN WE BE SAVED WITHOUT THE HOLY GHOST?

The Disciples at Ephesus

"**H**ave you received the Holy Ghost since you believed?**"** This question is recorded in Acts 19:2, and has been misunderstood by many believers. So the question we need answered would be, what *really* took place at Ephesus in Acts 19:1-6?

To start, we need to identify to whom Paul was asking this question. Verse 1 declares that he had found certain disciples and in verse 3 we discover that they were John the Baptist's disciples: "**And he said unto them, Unto what then were ye baptized? And they said, Unto John's baptism.**" We don't know why they hadn't heard of Jesus' ministry. Perhaps they had gotten lost in the chaos, or perhaps they fled for fear, considering the martyring of John. Whatever the case may have been, these disciples were *not* the disciples of Jesus – they had never encountered the ministry of Jesus, the Anointed One.

Later, in Acts 18:24-28, we find a preacher who was eloquent, mighty in the Scriptures, instructed in the way of the Lord and fervent in the spirit, but only knew the baptism of John (v.24-25). In other words, this preacher had not heard of the message of Jesus – the message of the Anointing. He knew only John the Baptist's message of repentance. He had not heard:

That word, I say, ye know, which was published throughout all Judea, and began from Galilee, after the baptism which John preached;

How God anointed Jesus of Nazareth with the Holy Ghost and with power: who went about doing good, and healing all that were oppressed of the devil; for God was with him.

—ACTS 10:37-38

But Aquila and Priscilla, two co-laborers with Paul, heard this man's teachings and were compelled to show him the way of God more perfectly (v.26). They mightily convinced him, by showing him the Scriptures, that Jesus is the Christ – the Anointed One (v.28).

The key statement that was made by these certain disciples at Ephesus was, **"We have not so much as <u>heard</u> whether there be any Holy Ghost"** (Acts 19:2, emphasis mine). The key word in this statement is "heard." They had not *heard* the message of the Holy Ghost – the power of Christ – the Anointed One. That's very significant when you consider Paul's letter to the Galatians. He asked, **"Received ye the Spirit by the works of the law, or by the hearing of faith?"** (Galatians 3:2). Paul was saying that we receive the Spirit by the hearing of faith. **"So then faith cometh by hearing, and hearing by the word of God"** (Romans 10:17). There was a lack of anointed Gospel preaching in Ephesus. How could these disciples receive the power of the Holy Ghost if they'd never heard that Word preached? Sadly, this same lack goes for many churches today, who are not preaching the truth of God's Word from the pulpit. That is why Paul declared, **"For I am not ashamed of the gospel of Christ: for *it* is the power of God unto salvation to every one that believeth; to the Jew first, and also the Greek"** (Romans 1:16, emphasis mine). The power of God that leads to salvation comes from the preaching of the Gospel of Christ!

Two Mistakes Regarding the Holy Ghost

There are two mistakes taught about the disciples at Ephesus, as recorded in Acts 19:2. The first mistake is to say that a born-again believer does not have the Holy Spirit. If you believe in Jesus the Son of God and that He died, was buried and rose again you have been sealed with the Holy Spirit.

The following verse will prove this to you:

In whom ye also trusted, after ye heard the word of truth, the gospel of your salvation: in whom also <u>after that ye believed</u>, ye were sealed with that Holy Spirit of promise.

—EPHESIANS 1:13
(emphasis mine)

Isn't it interesting that Paul would write this to the Ephesians, considering what had transpired in Ephesus a little earlier in his ministry? Notice what he says—after you heard and believed the word, you were sealed with that Holy Spirit of promise. There should be no confusion about which spirit he's referring to, because he uses the wording "that Holy Spirit of promise" – the one that was promised! Jesus said in Acts 1:4-5, **"wait for the promise of the Father, which, saith he, ye have heard of me. For John truly baptized with water, but ye shall be baptized with the Holy Ghost not many days hence.***"

But just because we have been sealed with the Holy Spirit doesn't mean that we are walking in the power of the fullness of the Holy Spirit. If every believer was Holy Ghost filled, then God would not have to instruct us to walk in the fullness of the Holy Ghost – it would be automatic. But through the following verses, we know this is not so:

Be not drunk with wine, wherein is excess; but be filled with the Spirit;

> **Speaking to yourselves in psalms and hymns and spiritual songs, singing and making melody in your heart to the Lord.**
> —EPHESIANS 5:18-19

Once again, in Paul's letter to those in Ephesus, he deals with the Holy Spirit. He told them in chapter 1 that they had been sealed with the Holy Spirit unto the day of redemption (v.13-14), and now here in Chapter 5 he commands them *"be filled with the Spirit"* (v.18). So there is a difference from being sealed and being filled. Every believer has been sealed, but that doesn't mean that they are walking in the fullness of the power of the Holy Ghost.

In Romans chapter 8, we read about how **"the law of the Spirit of life in Christ Jesus hath made me free from the law of sin and death"** (v.2). This chapter deals with our new life in Christ. Verse 9 says: **"Now if any man have not the Spirit of Christ, he is none of his."** This Scripture makes it clear that you cannot be saved and not have the Spirit. This is exactly what Jesus taught about the new birth, or being born again. Jesus credited the Spirit for the work of being born again in John 3.

> **Jesus answered, Verily, verily, I say unto thee, Except a man be born of water and of the Spirit, he cannot enter into the kingdom of God.**
> **That which is born of the flesh is flesh; and that which is born of the Spirit is spirit.**
> **Marvel not that I said unto thee, Ye must be born again.**
> —JOHN 3:5-7

Sadly, this passage of Scriptures has been incorrectly taught to mean water baptism, even though baptism is never mentioned at all in this chapter. The subject here is to be born again—born in the flesh and then born in the Spirit. Our natural birth is a birth of water. Anyone that knows anything about pregnancy and delivery can testify that a child is born of water. I can remember, with my own wife's pregnancies, that, as soon as her water broke, our children

21

were born. Nicodemus' own words further clear this up when he said, **"How can a man be born when he is old? Can he enter the second time into his mother's womb, and be born?"** (v. 4) Jesus said, **"That which is born of the flesh is flesh; and that which is born of the Spirit is spirit. Marvel not that I said unto thee, Ye must be born again"** (v. 6-7). So we can see that this passage of Scripture is referring to spiritual rebirth, salvation and redemption, and not water baptism. Further evidence of the work of the Holy Ghost in the work of redemption is found in Titus 3:5, **"Not by works of righteousness which we have done, but according to his mercy he saved us, by the washing of regeneration, and renewing of the Holy Ghost."** Later in this chapter, we will study further scriptural proof concerning the indwelling of the Holy Spirit at the same time of one's belief in Christ.

The second error that is often taught, regarding the disciples of John at Ephesus, is to assume that we do not truly possess the Holy Ghost unless we speak with tongues. We covered this misinterpretation in great detail in Chapter 1. There are many accounts of individuals who were filled with the Holy Ghost, but did not speak in tongues. John was **"filled with the Holy Ghost, even from his mother's womb"** (Luke 1:15), but he never spoke in tongues. **"Elisabeth was filled with the Holy Ghost"** (Luke 1:41). There is no account of her speaking in tongues. **"Zacharias was filled with the Holy Ghost"** (Luke 1:67). There is no account of him speaking in tongues. It was said of Barnabas in Acts 11:22-24, **"For he was a good man, and full of the Holy Ghost and faith: and much people were added unto the Lord."** There is no mention of him speaking in tongues. Stephen, Philip, Prochorus, Nicanor, Timon, Parmenas and Nicolas, the first deacons, were full of the Holy Ghost according to Acts 6:5, but there is no mention of them speaking in tongues.

There are other evidences of being filled with the Spirit. We read in Ephesians 5:18 that singing spiritual songs was a sign of being filled with the Spirit. Acts 4:31 declares that speaking the Word of God with boldness is evidence of being filled with the Spirit. It is a grave misconception to believe that speaking in tongues is the only sign of receiving the filling of the Holy Spirit.

Of the 40 men used by the Holy Spirit in authoring the books of the Bible, only three even mention speaking in tongues (Mark, Luke and Paul). Of the 27 books in the New Testament, there are only three books that make any reference to the gift of tongues (Mark, Acts, and 1 Corinthians). These are amazing facts, considering how some have taught that we are not saved unless we speak in tongues. If that were so, we have to believe that something so important would show up more in Scripture. As a matter of fact, if you search a list of all the conversions you see in the Book of Acts you will find thirty-one occurrences (Acts 2:41, 47, 4:4, 5:14, 6:1, 7, 8:12, 36-39, 9:17-20, 31, 35, 42, 11:21, 24, 13:12, 48, 14:1, 21, 16:5, 14-15, 29-34, 17:4, 12, 34, 18:8, 19:18, 28:24). Of the thirty-one conversions that included as many as five-thousand men at one time, you will only see the Gift of Tongues accompanying salvation on three occasions (Acts 2:1-4, 10:44-48, 19:6)! The point is, that if we give priority to what God gives priority, and search the New Testament of His Word, we will see, without confusion, that His will is that all men be saved, and that salvation comes only through faith in Jesus Christ. Many years ago I heard a pastor say that if you have not been filled with the Holy Spirit with the evidence of speaking in tongues, then you are not saved. He was then asked, "What about Billy Graham? He doesn't speak in tongues and has led millions to Christ." This pastor responded, "Billy Graham is not saved!" It is an absolute heresy to teach that salvation rests in one's ability to speak in tongues! Think of the multitudes of individuals who then would be lost if this false doctrine were true. Salvation rests in the finished work of Jesus Christ and our faith in Him!

What Is The Baptism, or Filling, of The Holy Ghost?

The word 'baptize' comes from two Greek words, **baptizo** and **bapto**, which means to immerse or to cover wholly. Jesus told his disciples in Acts 1:8, that they would receive power after the Holy Ghost comes upon them. This is known as the "baptism of the Holy Ghost". The word you need to notice in the verse is *upon*. It is a compound word, which means up and on. The Holy Ghost would come "up *and* on" them. We call this the anointing of the Spirit that empowers the believer to do the work of Jesus, the Anointed One. In Luke 4:18, Jesus declared, **"the Spirit of the Lord is upon me, because he hath anointed me to preach the gospel to the poor; he hath sent me to heal the broken hearted, to preach deliverance to the captives, and recovering of sight to the blind, to set at liberty them that are bruised***"* (Luke 4:18). You see, Jesus did not work any miracles or accomplish any work of the ministry until the Spirit of God came up and on Him—anointed or baptized Him—to do the work he was called to do. When one is baptized or anointed with the Holy Ghost, they are empowered to preach the Gospel of Christ (the Anointed One and His anointing). The Holy Ghost 'rubs off on' or anoints the believer with the burden removing, yoke destroying, power of God (Isaiah 10:27).

The Holy Spirit manifests Himself through a variety of spiritual gifts to build up and equip the church, to demonstrate the validity of the resurrection, and to confirm the power of the Gospel. The Bible's list of these gifts is not necessarily exhaustive, and the gifts may occur in various combinations. All believers are commanded to earnestly desire the manifestation of the best gifts in their lives (1 Corinthians 12:31). These gifts always operate in harmony with the Scriptures and should never be used in violation of Biblical parameters (Hebrews 2:4; Romans 1:11; 12:4-8; Ephesians 4:16; 2 Timothy 1:5-6; 1 Timothy 4:14; 1 Corinthians 12:1-31, 14:1-40; 1 Peter 4:10-11).

> **God also bearing them witness, both with signs and wonders, and with divers miracles, and gifts of the Holy Ghost, according to his own will?**
> **—HEBREWS 2:4**

> **For as we have many members in one body, and all members have not the same office:**
> **So we, being many, are one body in Christ, and every one members one of another.**

Having then gifts differing according to the grace that is given to us, whether prophecy, let us prophesy according to the proportion of faith;

Or ministry, let us wait on our ministering: or he that teacheth, on teaching;

Or he that exhorteth, on exhortation: he that giveth, let him do it with simplicity; he that ruleth, with diligence; he that sheweth mercy, with cheerfulness.
—ROMANS 12:4-8

As every man hath received the gift, even so minister the same one to another, as good stewards of the manifold grace of God.

If any man speak, let him speak as the oracles of God; if any man minister, let him do it as of the ability which God giveth: that God in all things may be glorified through Jesus Christ, to whom be praise and dominion for ever and ever. Amen.
—1 PETER 4:10-11

The Baptism of the Spirit was given at Pentecost and is the promise of the Father, sent by Jesus after His Ascension, to empower the Church to preach the Gospel throughout the whole earth (Joel 2:28-29; Matthew 3:11; Mark 16:17; Acts 1:5; 2:1-4, 17, 38-39; 8:14-17; 10:38, 44-47; 11:15-17; 19:1-6).

And it shall come to pass afterward, that I will pour out my spirit upon all flesh; and your sons and your daughters shall prophesy, your old men shall dream dreams, your young men shall see visions:

And also upon the servants and upon the handmaids in those days will I pour out my spirit.
—JOEL 2:28-29

The Fruit of the Spirit

The first law, or order, of God found in Scripture comes from Genesis 1:11, where God ordained that everything He created has the ability to reproduce more of its own kind. Not only did He create nature to reproduce itself, He ordained that every seed would produce another of "**its own kind.**" Simply put, the seed from a lemon will not produce an apple. Let's consider this law in relationship to the Holy Spirit, the Word of God and the Christian Faith. Many have placed much emphasis on the gifts of the Spirit without ever dealing with the importance and validity of the fruit of the Spirit. Jesus taught that a tree would be known by its fruit (Matthew 12:33).

Let's first gain a basic understanding of the laws of sowing and reaping. As we have already discovered, every seed will produce more of its "own kind" according to Genesis 1:11. The New Testament reiterates this law in Galatians 6:7, "**Be not deceived; God is not mocked: for whatsoever a man soweth, that shall he also reap.**" Therefore, if we don't want to harvest something in our lives, we must not sow it into our lives!

The next principle that we must put into practice is to identify the Word of God as a seed. In the Parable of the Sower, Jesus identified the seed as the Word when He said, "**Now the parable is this: The seed is the word of God**" (Luke 8:11). 1 Peter 1:23 says, "**Being born again, not of corruptible seed, but of incorruptible, by the word of God, which liveth and abideth for ever.**" God intends that the seed of His Word yield fruit in our lives. Notice Luke 8:15, "**But that on the good ground are they, which in an honest and good heart, having heard the word, keep it, and bring forth fruit with patience.**" It is obvious that there is a relationship between the Word of God in our lives and our being fruitful:

> **Now ye are clean through the word which I have spoken unto you.**
>
> **Abide in me, and I in you. As the branch cannot bear fruit of itself, except it abide in the vine; no more can ye, except ye abide in me.**

I am the vine, ye are the branches: He that abideth in me, and I in him, the same bringeth forth much fruit: for without me ye can do nothing.
—JOHN 15:3-5

It appears that many in the Body of Christ have forgotten the importance of "the fruit of the Spirit." Many are so caught up in the 'hype' of spiritual things that they have forgotten the needful things. What did Jesus say about being fruitful? How important is it that we bare spiritual fruit? Does the Bible define the fruit of the Spirit? In the remaining portion of this section, we will search the Word and answer these questions.

Every believer is called to bear spiritual fruit, because Jesus said that we would be known by our fruits:

Even so every good tree bringeth forth good fruit; but a corrupt tree bringeth forth evil fruit.

A good tree cannot bring forth evil fruit, neither can a corrupt tree bring forth good fruit.

Every tree that bringeth not forth good fruit is hewn down, and cast into the fire.

Wherefore by their fruits ye shall know them.
—MATTHEW 7:17-20

In addition to being known by our fruits, Proverbs 11:30 says, **"The fruit of the righteous is a tree of life; and he that winneth souls is wise."** This verse teaches us that our bearing fruit will enable us to win souls for Christ. The lost and hurting world isn't drawn to Christ by our super-spirituality or by a display of speaking in ecstatic utterances (tongues), but, rather, by the fruits of love, joy and peace. With that being said, let's look at the nine fruit of the Spirit as listed in the Bible.
—GALATIANS 5:22-23

We see that the first fruit that is listed is love. Jesus said, **"By this shall all men know that ye are my disciples, if ye have love one to another"** (John 13:35). There is a first-fruit principle in Scripture.

Romans 11:16 teaches us, **"For if the firstfruit be holy, the lump is also holy."** It is my conviction that if a believer does not walk in love, they will not see the other fruits of the Spirit in their lives. Love is the first-fruit; it is holy! Jesus taught that the whole law hung on our love for God and love for our neighbor (Matthew 22:38-40).

But possessing the fruit of the Spirit goes beyond just having love for our neighbors. There are *nine* fruit of the Spirit. In Scripture, the number nine represents 'judgment.' Judgment comes from the word **bema**, which is basically a platform of recognition - where one is recognized for good or for evil. We all are judged, or recognized, daily by those we come in contact with. As Christians, we should be recognized as such by all the fruit of the Spirit that is yielded in our lives.

I also believe that the nine fruit of the Spirit listed in Galatians 5:22-23 can be broken into groups of three. I am convinced that by breaking these fruit into groups of three, we discover how they relate to God, man and ourselves - upward, outward and inward. Allow me to explain this.

UPWARD - The first three fruit of the Spirit are *Love, Joy* and *Peace* - all of these are directed towards God.

OUTWARD - The second group of three is *Longsuffering, Gentleness* and *Goodness* - these are directed towards man.

INWARD - The third and final group of three is *Faith, Meekness* and *Temperance* - these are exercised within.

Based on all that we've studied thus far, I hope you can see that it is impossible to yield fruit of the 'God-kind' without a seed of the 'God-kind'. And the Word of God is the seed that will produce the fruit of the Spirit!

Out of His Belly Shall Flow Rivers of Living Water

I once attended a church service where the minister requested that hands be laid on certain candidates' stomachs (or bellies) in order, that they might receive the Holy Ghost. I've also talked to many other believers who have witnessed similar situations. Why do we see this so often? Is this scriptural? Let's move deeper into our study and see what the Word has to say about such practices.

In the last day, that great day of the feast, Jesus stood and cried, saying, If any man thirst, let him come unto me and drink.
He that believeth on me, as the scripture hath said, out of his belly shall flow rivers of living water.
(But this he spake of the Spirit, which they that believe on him should receive: for the Holy Ghost was not yet given; because Jesus was not yet glorified.
—JOHN 7:37-39

Let's begin by defining the word 'belly.' It means 'the center of one's being.' This does not mean the literal stomach, but the spirit of a man. Man is a spirit, he lives in a body and possesses a soul (1 Thessalonians 5:23). The center of our being is our spirit. The Holy Spirit does not reside in our stomach! It would be foolish to believe so. We are the temple of the Spirit of God, and He resides in our spirit man.

Next, we must recognize who receives this 'living water,' which is the Holy Spirit— "**he that believeth on me.**" So this tells us that, if we believe on Jesus, from our spirit will flow the power of the Holy Spirit. Our spirit becomes His dwelling place from the moment we believe. Jesus has been glorified (John 17) and the Holy Spirit has been sent (Acts 2:1-4, Ephesians 4:8-10). And as believers, we have the promise of His indwelling. But, there is a difference between the Holy Spirit *residing* in us and the Holy Spirit *presiding*.

At the time that Jesus spoke these words, notice what the Scripture says: "**for the Holy Ghost was not yet given; because Jesus was not yet glorified.**" You see, today, Jesus *has already* been glorified.

He has ascended and His Spirit has been sent. There is now no need to wait for the Holy Spirit! So now, upon our belief, we can see the instant manifestation of what Jesus said! **"He that believeth on me, as the scripture hath said, out of his belly shall flow rivers of living water"** (John 7:38).

Chapter 3

WHAT DOES THE WORD OF GOD SAY ABOUT PRAYING IN AN UNKNOWN TONGUE?

Popular Opinion

I was once confronted by a lady who asked me to pray for her, but when I asked her what her request was, she said, "Just pray in tongues. The English language won't do." Under the instruction of a broad number of ministers, believers are spending large amounts of their prayer time speaking a language that no one understands, including the one doing the praying! One might encounter in many different churches, denominations and locations such practices – ecstatic, unintelligible sounds coming forth from the mouths of people throughout the assembly – all proclaiming that they are praying in tongues or in the Spirit.

What does all this mean? Does the Bible teach such a practice? In this chapter, we are going to search the Scriptures and see what God's Word has to say about 'praying in tongues' and His instruction on prayer. Is there really a method by which we speak directly to God without understanding what we have said? Does the Holy Spirit utter words from our mouth that are beyond our comprehension? Many have their opinions, but the Word of God has the Truth!

Paul's Letter to the Corinthians

The foundational teaching of praying in tongues or 'praying in the spirit' is based on the writings of Paul in 1 Corinthians 14. Before we study the Scriptures written in this chapter, let's take a look at this church that Paul is writing to, and what is found in the content of this letter. When we read the Book of First Corinthians, it is vital that we realize that it is a book of rebuke. Paul is *scolding* a carnal church. The following is a list of things that he admonished the church of Corinth about in each chapter of I Corinthians:

Chapter 1 – for strife and division
Chapter 2 – for being naturally minded
Chapter 3 – for being carnality, jealousy, strife and divisions
Chapter 4 – for being proud and puffed up
Chapter 5 – for condoning immorality
Chapter 6 – for going to the law against one another
Chapter 7 – for lack of order in their homes
Chapter 8 – for idolatry
Chapter 9 – for not providing for the ministers of the gospel
Chapter 10 – for fellowshipping with devils
Chapter 11 – for heresies and abusing the Lord's Supper
Chapter 12 – for schisms in the body and the abuse of spiritual gifts
Chapter 13 – for lacking love
Chapter 14 – for a lack of order in the church
Chapter 15 – for denying the resurrection
Chapter 16 – for unfaithfulness in financial stewardship

This doesn't sound like the church that we should be patterning our Christian walk after! This was, by no means, the model church. It seems safe to say that a church that used the Lord's Supper to satisfy their appetite and to indulge in drink is *not* the kind of church we should be using as an example (1 Corinthians 11:20-22)!

Corinth was a major trade center, which meant there was a constant flow of many dialects of believers passing through the city. Many of these visitors didn't understand the native tongue or dialect of Corinth. These visitors to the church at Corinth would speak out or even pray without an interpreter, not considering that no one was able to understand them. Paul deals with this confusion in chapter 14, where the word 'tongues' appears fifteen times. Many have been programmed to assume that this term, 'tongues', refers to some ecstatic, unknown prayer language; but that is not the meaning of this word, nor the context in which Paul is writing. There are four things that Paul deals with in chapter 14:

Tongues and public speaking (1 Corinthians 14:1-13)
Tongues and public prayer (1 Corinthians 14:14-20)
Tongues and public prophecy (1 Corinthians 14:21-22)
Tongues and public worship (1 Corinthians 14:23-40)

Praying In Tongues

Let's study the verses of Scripture from which the doctrine of 'praying in tongues' is taught. The most popular is found in 1 Corinthians 14:14, **"For if I pray in an *unknown* tongue, my spirit prayeth, but my understanding is unfruitful."** In the King James Bible, anytime we see a word in *italic*, it means that word was added by the translators and was not found in the original writings. The word *'unknown'* is always in italic throughout chapter 14 of Paul's first letter to the Corinthians. That word was added by privilege of the translators to help you to understand the context. The word 'tongue' in these verses of Scripture is translated from the Greek word *glossa*, which means language or dialect. There is no "unknown" tongue, by definition of language itself. Every language is understood by someone – that's what makes it a language, else you speak barbarian.

There are, it may be, so many kinds of voices in the world, and none of them is without signification.
Therefore if I know not the meaning of the voice, I shall be unto him that speaketh a barbarian, and he that speaketh shall be a barbarian unto me.
—1 CORINTHIANS 14:10-11
(emphasis mine)

The implication of Paul's instruction was that the language was *"unknown"* to other dialects of people who were present in the assembly, simply because it was not their native language, and they therefore could not understand it. For an example, if a Spanish speaking individual prayed in my presence, his understanding is unfruitful or unproductive to me seeing that I only speak English and have no knowledge of the Spanish dialect. Therefore, in his prayer, he is only communicating with God, because I don't understand him. So, I can neither agree with his prayer by saying "amen," nor be edified by his prayer, because I don't understand his tongue or dialect. That's exactly what Paul is saying.

What is it then? I will pray with the spirit, and I will pray with the understanding also: I will sing with the spirit, and I will sing with the understanding also.

Else when thou shalt bless with the spirit, how shall he that occupieth the room of the unlearned say Amen at thy giving of thanks, seeing he understandeth not what thou sayest?

For thou verily givest thanks well, but the other is not edified.

— 1 CORINTHIANS 14:15-17

There are some truths here that we *must* understand. Notice, in the phrase, **"pray with the spirit,"** that the word 'spirit' is not capitalized – therefore it can not be referring to the Holy Spirit, or else it would be capitalized. As we saw earlier, the Bible teaches that man is a spirit, and that he lives in a body and possesses a soul. The center of our being is our spirit. Jesus said, in John 6:63, that the words He speaks are spirit. Words are spiritual containers that carry messages to the hearer - God hears and knows every dialect!

Notice that the man praying 'in the spirit' knew what he was praying. He was giving thanks to God. This one praying isn't lacking understanding of what he is saying – he knows exactly what he is saying but the one that occupies the room, in his presence, has no idea what he is praying because he has no knowledge of his dialect. Paul says that in such a case, the unlearned can't say "amen" at the offering of that prayer. Notice the word 'unlearned.' This refers to the individual who has not learned that particular language, tongue or dialect of the one praying; so he is unable to give agreement to the prayer that was offered up. So the one speaking is not confused about what he has said, but, rather, the one *listening* is confused. This isn't a lesson on some ecstatic prayer language that no one understands. Paul is adamantly saying either pray in a language (tongue) that the congregation understands, seek an interpreter or speak only to God privately.

Allow me to try and explain this even further. I believe that many have been taught that the one praying has no understanding of his prayer language. Let's look again at the verse that has confused so many. **"For if I pray in an unknown tongue, my spirit prayeth, <u>but my understanding is unfruitful</u>"** (1 Corinthians 14:14, emphasis mine). Some have concluded that phrase to mean the individual does not understand his own language. But that is not what this verse is saying, when you read it in context. The one praying (in another dialect) knows what he's praying or singing, etc. However, because those present with him in the church do not know his dialect, he's unable to share his knowledge.

Let me give you an example. Some time ago, I was in a position to be a blessing to a Hispanic family. When I contacted the father with an opportunity that would have benefitted him, his wife and child, I discovered that he was very limited in his understanding of the English language. It was very frustrating for me to have a solution to a crisis that he faced and not have the ability to share my knowledge. I knew what I could offer him. I had total understanding of what he needed and what I could do. However, my understanding was not fruitful, or productive–not because I didn't know what I was saying, but because he did not know my dialect.

So now we can see that, in the context of Paul's instruction in chapter 14, he is not talking about some unknown, ecstatic utterance, but the speaking of a literal dialect that is foreign to those who haven't learned it. If Paul reproves this prayer, which is a legitimate language, for its use among those who haven't learned it, imagine what he would say about the prayers in ecstatic, barbarian-like utterances!

So likewise ye, except ye utter by the tongue words easy to be understood, how shall it be known what is spoken? For ye shall speak into the air.
— 1 CORINTHIANS 14:9

That's not to say that the one praying is not edified, but that his words are lost in the air if the hearer does not know the language spoken. Look at Paul's explanation:

But if there be no interpreter, let him keep silence in the church; and let him speak to himself, and to God.
— 1 CORINTHIANS 14:28

Paul emphasizes that the languages spoken need to be understood by the hearers, or else the one who desires to share the mysteries of the Gospel needs to sit quietly and meditate between himself and God. He gives clear instruction. Notice these statements:

> **Now brethren if I come unto you speaking with tongues, what shall I profit you, except I shall speak to you either by revelation, or by knowledge, or by prophesying, or by doctrine?**
>
> **And even things without life giving sound, whether pipe or harp, except they give a distinction in the sounds, how shall it be known what is piped or harped?**
>
> **For if the trumpet give an uncertain sound, who shall prepare himself to the battle?**
>
> **So likewise ye, except ye utter by the tongue words easy to be understood, how shall it be known what is spoken? For ye shall speak into the air.**
>
> **Yet in the church I had rather speak five words with my understanding, that by my voice I might teach others also, than ten thousand words in an unknown tongue.**
>
> **If any man speaks in an unknown tongue, let it be by two, or at the most by three, and that by course; and let one interpret.**

But if there be no interpreter, let him keep silence in the church; and let him speak to himself, and to God.
— 1 CORINTHIANS 14:6-9, 19,
27, 28

Sometimes I am in absolute awe of how far out of context my friends and fellow laborers in the faith have taken this instruction. It's very difficult for me to understand how someone can take this simple instruction regarding tongues in a public assembly, and use it to justify ecstatic babblings!

I'm hard-pressed to believe that an individual could spend time reading the Word of God, and come across anything in the entire Bible that would lead them to stop praying their own language and to begin praying in an ecstatic, meaningless utterance, with the belief that this is the only way to ensure that his or her prayers are heard by God. I honestly do not believe it possible that a believer could come to this conclusion without having heard someone else pray in this manner, or without having been influenced in some way to stop praying as Jesus instructs us (Matthew 6:9-17) and to begin to adapt to the idea of an unrecognizable "prayer language." It's impossible to even find the words 'prayer' and 'language' written together anywhere in the canon of Scripture! One *can*, however, read the Word of God and discover a need for repentance, salvation, faith, healing and deliverance. One *can* read the Bible and gain an understanding of Jesus, heaven, hell, the devil, prophecy and the end-times. Scripture *does* gives insight on God's will for marriage, family, raising children and stewardship. But I have found no evidence that anyone can read the Bible and draw the conclusion that they need to begin to utter babblings or ecstatic and repetitive sounds and call it a prayer language.

Some years ago I got a call from a young man who was away at a Bible college. He called me on behalf of his roommate, who was very distraught about a church service they had attended that night. There had been a minister there who preached on 'tongues,' and the importance of a believer receiving his or her "prayer language." He informed the congregation that unless they prayed in an unknown tongue, their prayers would be hindered by Satan. After the message, he had an altar call where he laid hands on those who wanted to receive the Holy Ghost with the evidence of speaking in tongues. This young man went forward to receive his prayer language. After many attempts of laying on of hands and prayer by the pastor, the young man still was unable to speak this unknown tongue that the pastor referred to as his prayer language.

When he and his roommates returned to the dorm that night, this young man was literally hysterical, wondering why God would withhold this gift from him, when he so desperately and sincerely sought it. He began questioning his salvation, and doubting whether he had even truly been called to be a preacher. This was the state of the situation when I received the call, and was asked to speak with the young man. He shared with me how he had been out in the streets and addicted to drugs before Christ came into his life. He shared how he had come from a broken home, and how Jesus had literally changed his life, from the inside out. His heart was broken for his parents, because he wanted them to come to know the power of Jesus, and the salvation He gives. He said that he had been praying for his family, but, based on what the minister told him, his prayers were being stopped by Satan because he was not using his prayer language. And now he was distraught to the point of wanting to give up his entire walk of faith and life, because he was unable to attain such a language.

I asked him the simple question, "How did you get saved?" He told me that he had attended a youth conference, and heard the Good News of Jesus Christ. I said, "No, what did you actually *do* to get saved besides go to the place where you heard the gospel?" He replied, "I went forward at the altar call." "But what did you do at the altar?" I asked. He said, "I called upon Jesus, and asked Him to save me and deliver me, and I confessed Him as the Lord of my life!" I replied, "And what tongue did you use?" He said, "What do you mean?" "What tongue – what language—did you pray to God in, to receive your salvation?" He said, "I prayed in English – the only one I know."

I went on to ask him more about his changed life and his salvation. In hearing his testimony, there was no doubt that Jesus had saved this young man from a life of abuse and destruction. Here was a young man who had not only been saved, but desired for others to receive the same life-changing power, and had devoted his life to the ministry. I then asked him this question, "If Satan was going to stop any prayer, or if he even *had* the power to stop your prayers, why didn't he stop that one – the one where you called upon the Lord to save you?" Immediately, the young man rejoiced! Satan doesn't possess the power to stop our prayers! If he did, no one could be saved! In John 14:14, Jesus said that whatever we ask of the Father, in *His* name, He would do it! I can tell that, by the time I hung up the phone, that young man was delivered. Yet sadly, there are an untold number of believers facing this very same dilemma each week. And it is for those, who seek the truth, that I am inspired to write this book.

Men of Other Tongues

I thank my God, I speak with tongues more than ye all. Yet in the church I had rather speak five words with my understanding, that by my voice I might teach others also, than ten thousand words in an unknown tongue.
— 1 CORINTHIANS 14:18-19

Many would use these Scriptures to say that even the apostle Paul "spoke in tongues." But we come to a different conclusion when we look at these verses in their context: Paul was multilingual, meaning he spoke *many* different languages. He said that he spoke many languages, but in the church he spoke the language that was understood so that he could teach others. He also said that five words that *can* be understood are better to be spoken than ten thousand words in a language (tongue) that is not known. What an amazing statement!

But why did Paul thank God that he spoke with tongues? Because, without that ability, he could not have spread the Gospel to other nations! And in Acts 22:2, his ability to speak Hebrew gave him the opportunity to testify of Jesus before the chief captain. Paul wasn't thankful for some ecstatic language, but was thankful for the ability to speak in many dialects or known languages, so that his message of the salvation of Jesus Christ could be understood by many. His missionary journeys took him through Asia Minor and into Europe and Greece. He traveled to Caesarea, Antioch in Syria, Galatia, Cyprus, Paphos, Pamphylia, Perga, Attalia, Derbe, Lystra, Iconium, Laodecia, Colosse, Antioch (in Pisidia), Miletus, Ephesus, Troas, Philippi, Athens, Thessalonica, Berea, Macedonia, Melita and Rome. How could he have been the world's greatest missionary had he not been fluent in many languages?

To get back to his letter to the church at Corinth and his instruction on tongues in 1 Corinthians 14, Paul is not referring to some ecstatic utterance, but foreign languages spoken in the presence of unlearned men. He emphasized the importance of understanding. Notice again what he said, **"Yet in the church I had rather speak five words with my understanding, that by my voice I might teach others also, than ten thousand words in an unknown tongue."** So, with this in mind, why do we see so many churches promote such confusing utterances to be spoken, and witness the total disregard of Paul's instruction in the Word of God and the importance of understanding?

I've heard it said to me on many occasions that the Word tells us **"forbid not to speak with tongues"** (1 Corinthians 14:39). This is correct but it needs to be understood within the context and definition of what 'tongues' are. This Scripture is telling us that if one is present within the assembly that does not speak the known language or dialect of those present, that he is not to be forbidden to speak. As we studied earlier, he can speak to himself or to God (1 Corinthians 14:28). But if he wishes to speak to the church he needs the interpretation (1 Corinthians 14:5, 13). There are many who seek verses of Scripture to endorse their practice. They receive one verse while rejecting another. You will never hear some quote 1 Corinthians 13:8, which declares, **"whether they be tongues, they shall cease."** I do not believe that we should use one verse of Scripture and then avoid another in an effort to support our own opinions or traditions. I do believe, however, that one can search *all* of the Scriptures related to tongues and walk away with clear understanding. But we have to be willing to allow the Bible to interpret itself, not add or take away from what it is saying and to see what Scripture is saying within its context. I was reading a "tongues book" written by a popular minister many years ago as a young Christian. I was in search of the truth and this book was given to me by a friend who wanted me to understand their church's practice of *prayer languages*. I was amazed at how many times this author would reference a portion of Scripture followed by "…" When I went and read the Scripture in its entirety it wasn't saying what he was conveying it to say. I do not believe in taking a position and then trying to find Bible verses to back up my opinion or practice. I believe in searching the Scriptures and allow our convictions to come from what God said! We do not change the Word to fit us; we change to fit the Word!

Many years ago I visited a church, and, while we were all seated listening to the pastor, a woman jumped to her feet and began to speak mantra-like, ecstatic words that many deem as *tongues*. After a few moments, another lady across the sanctuary jumped to her feet and she said that God had given her the interpretation. She then began to express to the congregation what the other woman had supposedly spoken in an unknown tongue. Wow! Now that seems really deep or super-spiritual doesn't it? However, if God wanted a word to be spoken to the congregation and we were all English-speaking individuals, couldn't He just have spoken the words through the first woman in English? If His Word says that in all of our getting we should get understanding (Proverbs 4:7), then I believe that He would have spoken through a *tongue* (language) that all who were present could understand. You may wonder why these things happen in some assemblies. I believe that it is simply the result of many being taught by a misunderstanding of what Paul instructed through the Word of God regarding speaking in a multi-dialect congregation.

I spoke to a Hispanic church some years ago. I had an interpreter who would listen to my English words and would then turn and share the message so that those who spoke Spanish could receive edification. If I did not have that interpreter, I should have remained quiet. I could have spoken to myself or to God. But my knowledge could not have benefitted those in the congregation that day if I couldn't share it in words that they could understand. As a matter of fact, I remember having to be selective with the words I used so that my interpreter wouldn't have to struggle to find Spanish words with the same meaning. It was better for them that I used fewer words that could be understood, than thousands that they could not understand. That's exactly what Paul was saying to the church at Corinth:

> **Yet in the church I had rather speak five words with my understanding, that by my voice I might teach others also, than ten thousand words in an unknown tongue.**
> **— 1 CORINTHIANS 14:19**

Had God never carried His gospel and saving grace to the Gentiles, neither the church at Corinth, nor any other assembly, would have had to worry about a multi-dialect crowd. None of the Old Testament prophets, or even Jesus himself, had to deal with an assembly of people that had a mixture of foreign tongues. The Jews were the chosen people of God. They were the only nation that had received the Word of God. But God broke down the partition of dialects on the Day of Pentecost, when Peter preached the message of Jesus, the Anointed One, and at least sixteen different dialects of people heard in their own language the wonderful works of God (Acts 2:11).

God had prophesied through the prophet Isaiah of the refreshing (sending of His Spirit), and how He would use men of other tongues to speak to His people, but they would not hear (Isaiah 28:11-12). Paul explains the 'tongues' issue to the Corinthians by quoting this prophesy:

> **In the law it is written, With men of other tongues and other lips will I speak unto this people; and yet for all that will they not hear me, saith the Lord. Wherefore tongues are for a sign, not to them that believe, but to them that believe not: but prophesying serveth not for them that believe not, but for them that believe.**
> **— 1 CORINTHIANS 14:21-22**

God used tongues as a sign to the unbelieving Jews, through the testimony of Jesus, that the Holy Ghost had been sent. The Gift of Tongues served not for the believing Gentiles, but rather the unbelieving Jews.

Notice Paul's remarks if we don't give heed to understand his exhortation:

> **If therefore the whole church be come together into one place, and all speak with tongues, and there come in those that are unlearned, or unbelievers, will they not say that ye are mad?**
>
> —1 CORINTHIANS 14:23

Paul said that if a man walked in that had not learned the dialects of all those speaking, he would walk away saying that those people are mad or crazy! Now, this is not referring to the ecstatic sounds that are spoken by so many. This is referring to chaos created by a multi-language assembly speaking at the same time. I have heard so many individuals tell me of horrifying experiences that they have had when surrounded by a bunch of people chattering strange sounds. Many have told me, "I'll never step foot in that church again, those people are crazy!" If I've heard it once, I've heard it a hundred times, and with each admission, my heart breaks.

> **If any man speak in an unknown tongue, let it be by two, or at the most by three, and that by course; and let one interpret. But if there be no interpreter, let him keep silence in the church; and let him speak to himself, and to God.**
>
> —1 CORINTHIANS 14:27-28

Here, Paul's instruction is that if there are those who wish to speak of different dialects or languages unknown to the assembly – it must be by course (they must take turns) and there must be an interpreter. If there is no one that can interpret the foreign language, then the foreigner must keep silence. He is allowed to speak to himself and to God (for only he and God know what he's saying). This

Scripture would make no sense if we look at it in the context with which many believers use it to justify speaking in an unintelligible language. Why would he speak to himself if he didn't know what he was saying? So we can see that is not what Paul was saying to the church. The truth is, it's not unusual for a person to speak to himself while in the spirit. David spoke to himself in Psalms 103:1-2 when he said, **"Bless the Lord, O my soul: and all that is within me, bless His holy name. Bless the Lord, O my soul: and forget not all His benefits."** Ephesians 5:18-20 says, **"And be not drunk with wine, wherein is excess; nut be filled with the Spirit; Speaking to yourselves in psalms and hymns and spiritual songs, singing and making melody in your heart to the Lord."** Notice who Paul said we should speak to - ourselves and God. We also see that in this instruction on being filled with the Spirit there is no mention of tongues.

Babel

We find diversities of tongues first mentioned as a curse that God placed on the children of men in Genesis 11:1-9. The earth at the time was of one language (v.1). God cursed these men for their evil imagination of building a tower to reach into heaven in defiance to His command that they should be fruitful and multiply and fill the whole earth. God confounded their language so that they were not able to understand one another's speech (v.7). Therefore, it was named "Babel" (v.9), because of their confounded or confusing language. The word Babel is defined as a place of noise and confusion: a confused sound or racket. Isn't it interesting that sounds which are confusing, or not able to be understood, were called a curse? Sadly enough, this is what is heard in so many assemblies, under the guise of godliness.

The Angelic Tongue

There are many that believe that they speak a heavenly language or an angelic tongue. I have been approached by some who have declared that they speak with tongues of angels, as Paul did. But, did Paul really speak with the tongues of angels? This belief is taken from 1 Corinthians 13:1-3, **"Though I speak with the tongues of men and of angels, and have not charity, I am become as sounding brass, or a tinkling cymbal.***"* Now, thus far it would appear that Paul speaks such a tongue, until you continue to read. Verses 2-3, **"And though I have the gift of prophecy, and understand all mysteries, and all knowledge; and though I have all faith, so that I could remove mountains, and have not charity, I am nothing. And though I bestow all my goods to feed the poor, and though I give my body to be burned, and have not charity, it profiteth me nothing."** When you read these verses in context you will see that the word "though" means "even if." For example, Paul also said in verse 2, **"though I have all faith,"** but he didn't have all faith. And in verse 3 he adds, *"***Though I give my body to be burned,***"* yet Paul was beheaded, not burned. So, it is obvious that the term "though" means "even if," when read in context.

The word "angels" in 1 Corinthians 13:1 is interpreted "messenger." That is one of the purposes of angels in the Bible – to deliver the Word of God. An angel spoke to Abraham in Genesis 22:11-12. The angel said, **"Abraham, Abraham: and he said, Here am I.***"* There doesn't seem to be a communication problem here and I'm sure Abraham was glad – for the angel told him not to sacrifice his son! An angel spoke to Joseph in Matthew 1:20 and told him to take Mary as his wife for the child she carried was conceived of the Holy Ghost; and she would bring forth a Son and that they should name the child JESUS. Joseph definitely understood the angel's message. In Luke 1:26-35, Mary was approached by an angel and was told she would conceive in her womb, and bring forth a son, and to call his name JESUS. In verses 34-35, we see Mary question the angel and the angel responding to her with the Word of God. No communication problem here! Angels spoke to the shepherds in Luke 1:10-14, and declared, **"I bring you good tidings of**

great joy," and gave them the news that Jesus had been born and where to find him. Once again, the people had no problem understanding the angel's messages. In John 20:12, two angels spoke with Mary at the empty tomb of Jesus. The Book of Revelation, written by John, was delivered to him by an angel. Revelation 1:1, "**The Revelation of Jesus Christ, which God gave unto him, to show unto his servants things which must shortly come to pass; and he sent and signified it by his angel unto his servant John: Who bare record of the word of God, and of the testimony of Jesus Christ, and of all the things that he saw.**" There is no account in the Bible of an angel speaking words that cannot be understood. Angels carry out and minister the Word of God! They are often used as the messengers of God, and God is not the author of confusion (1 Corinthians 14:33).

We can conclude, with fair certainty, that, if these angels sounded like what we hear in common church assemblies, then Isaac might be dead, Joseph may not have married Mary, Mary may not have received the Word of God, Jesus may not have been born, and John would not have been able to write the Book of Revelation!

They Shall Speak With New Tongues

One of the foundation verses for the tongues teaching is taken from the Gospel of Mark:

> **And he said unto them, Go ye into all the world, and preach the gospel to every creature. He that believeth and is baptized shall be saved; but he that believeth not shall be damned. And these signs shall follow them that believe; In my name shall they cast out devils; they shall speak with new tongues; They shall take up serpents; and if they drink any deadly thing, it shall not hurt them; they shall lay hands on the sick, and they shall recover.**
> —MARK 16:15-18

Jesus lists the signs that will follow the believers. First of all, it is a mistake to think that all of these signs would follow all believers. If that were so, then we would see each one of these signs in the life of every believer. This is a general statement made by Jesus referring to the signs that would soon appear.

Before we discuss the "new tongues" Jesus is referring to, let's first deal with the other signs: casting out devils, taking up serpents, drinking of a deadly thing without hurt, laying hands on the sick and seeing them recover. We see these signs manifest throughout the Book of Acts. Jesus places no emphasis on any one sign. For someone to say that all believers should speak in new tongues, they would have to also say that all believers should cast out devils, take up serpents, drink deadly poison without harm, lay hands on the sick and see them recover. Jesus is declaring the types of signs that would immediately follow His disciples' preaching of the gospel.

In Acts 28:1-6, Paul was bit by a viper and in verse 5, the Bible declares, **"And he shook off the beast into the fire, and felt no harm."** In Acts 8:5-7, Philip cast out devils and healed the sick. Verse 7 says, **"For unclean spirits, crying with loud voice, came out of many that were possessed with them: and many taken with palsies, and that were lame, were healed."** And in Acts 2:4, we see the gift of tongues manifest – breaking the language barrier for as many as sixteen dialects of people!

> **Now when this was noised abroad, the multitude came together, and were confounded, because that <u>every man heard them speak in his own language</u>. And they were all amazed and marveled, saying one to another, Behold, are not all these which speak Galileans?**
>
> **And how hear we every man in our own tongue, wherein we were born?**
>
> —ACTS 2:7-8 (emphasis mine)

This was no muttering of words without meaning! Peter wasn't chattering out words that no one could understand. He was preaching the Word of God and because of the gift of Tongues, his words were understood by all that heard him.

It's amazing to me how far out of context many have taken the gift of tongues. Instead of recognizing it as the way for God to spread His word to every dialect, breaking the language barriers – many have made it to be the speaking of some incomprehensible language that no one understands. But the truth remains that the only time the gift of tongues is associated with the outpouring of the Holy Spirit in the Word of God is when there was a communication barrier caused by people from more than one language group who were all gathered together in one place.

In Acts 4:31 you have a repeat experience described in Acts 2. They prayed and the place was shaken and they were filled with the Holy Ghost, but because there were no foreigners present, the gift of tongues was not present. "**And when they had prayed, the place was shaken where they were assembled together; and they were all filled with the Holy Ghost, and they spake the word of God with boldness.**" The purpose of the baptism of the Holy Spirit is for power to preach the Word!

<u>Tongues of Fire</u>

And when the day of Pentecost was fully come, they were all with one accord in one place.

And suddenly there came a sound from heaven as of a rushing mighty wind, and it filled all the house where they were sitting.

And there appeared unto them cloven tongues like as fire, and it sat upon each of them.

And they were all filled with the Holy Ghost, and began to speak with other tongues, as the Spirit gave them utterance.

—ACTS 2:1-4

Fire is a symbol of power. God gave this gift in the form of tongues of fire so they would know that He would *empower* their feeble tongues, just as he did to Moses when he went before Pharaoh in Exodus 4:10-12, and to Isaiah, when he touched his lips with a coal from the heavenly altar in Isaiah 6:6-7.

I once read a church brochure where all were invited to attend a service where "every Sunday is like Pentecost!" This advertisement is just another example of some inaccuracies that continue to be perpetuated in churches by sincere believers who are ignorant to the truth that is in God's Word. *Pentecost* means fiftieth. The day of Pentecost was a Jewish holy day that came fifty days after Passover, when Christ was offered *once* for our sins (Hebrews 10:12). So, Pentecost cannot be a continuing event. The Promise of the Father has already come - the Holy Ghost has been sent! The Spirit of Truth resides in the Body of Christ and He has empowered us to preach the Gospel as we await the glorious appearing of our Lord Jesus Christ! Devoted Israelites would come from all over the Roman Empire to worship in Jerusalem. God chose this opportunity, at this appointed time, to bestow the gift of tongues upon the disciples; it gave them the ability to preach the gospel of Jesus to all nations that were present on the day of Pentecost. As we learned in previous chapters, many different dialects would be represented that day (Acts 2:9-11)! And each nation heard their native language as the disciples proclaimed God's Word (Acts 2:7). As a result of this empowering by the Holy Spirit, thousands were converted, and were able to return to their respective lands carrying the message of faith in Jesus! This fulfills Jesus' words in Acts 1:8, **"But ye shall receive power after that the Holy Ghost is come upon you: and ye shall be witnesses unto to me both in Jerusalem, and in all Judea, and in Samaria, and unto the uttermost part of the earth."**

The Bible specifically states that not only was there a miracle with every dialect being able to understand the words of Peter (a Jew) through the gift of tongues, but also there appeared upon them **"cloven tongues like as of fire."** The word *cloven* means split or divided. God divided the words spoken into every dialect present so that all could receive the message of the Gospel of Jesus Christ! Notice what the Amplified Bible says:

And there appeared to them tongues resembling fire, which were separated and distributed and which settled on each one of them.

And they were all filled (diffused throughout their souls) with the Holy Spirit and began to speak in other (different, foreign) languages (tongues), as the Spirit kept giving them clear and loud expression [in each tongue in appropriate words].

—ACTS 2:3-4, Amplified Bible

God further demonstrated this miraculous event with what appeared to be fire that sat upon each of them. Can you imagine seeing such an awesome manifestation? What a glorious sight that must have been!

Chapter 4

WHAT DOES THE BIBLE SAY ABOUT PRAYING IN THE HOLY SPIRIT?

Agreement with the Father, the Word and the Holy Ghost: Prayers that Get Results

God uses an analogy of heaven and earth to compare his thoughts to ours:

> **For my thoughts are not your thoughts, neither are your ways my ways, saith the Lord.**
> **For as the heavens are higher than the earth, so are my ways higher than your ways, and my thoughts than your thoughts.**
> —ISAIAH 55:8-9

This means that when we pray, we need to agree with the thoughts that God has toward us - thoughts that are settled in heaven. The Bible tells us exactly what God has said that are His thoughts towards us.

> **For I know the thoughts that I think toward you, saith the Lord, thoughts of peace, and not evil, to give you an expected end.**
> **Then shall ye call upon me, and ye shall go and pray unto me, and I will hearken unto you.**
> —JEREMIAH 29:11-12

Look at God's instruction to believers:

> **Seek ye out of the book of the Lord and read: no one of these shall fail, none shall want her mate: for my mouth it hath commanded, and his spirit it hath gathered them.**
> —ISAIAH 34:16

This verse makes God's desire for us abundantly clear. He's challenging us to seek His Word and make demands on it in prayer. He says that whatever Words His mouth has spoken, His Spirit will gather them and manifest them! When we declare the Word of God, the Holy Ghost moves immediately to bring those words to pass! God spoke on Creation's dawn, "**Let there be light**," and the Spirit of God moved to manifest the light (Genesis 1:1-3). The Holy Spirit has always, and *will* always, work with the Word of God. They are in total agreement – working as one.

Now let's take a look at a verse that has been misunderstood, by some, to tell us to use some type of unknown, incomprehensible, barbarian-like prayer language when we go before God. But we are going to rightly divide the Word, and gain a clear understanding of its true meaning:

> **But ye, beloved, building up yourselves on your most holy faith, praying in the Holy Ghost.**
> — JUDE 20

Let's study this verse carefully. According to this Scripture, when I pray in the Holy Ghost, it increases my faith. And what does the Bible say about faith? "**So then faith cometh by hearing, and hearing by the word of God**" (Romans 10:17). 1 John 5:7 declares,

"There are three that bear record in heaven, the Father, the Word, and the Holy Ghost: and these three are one." Therefore, according to God's Word, which is the final authority, the Holy Ghost is in perfect oneness with the Word. We could say, then, that praying *in the Holy Ghost* is the same as praying *in the Word of God.* That makes complete agreement between the Father, His Word and His Holy Spirit. And since we know that faith comes by hearing the Word of God, we are building up our faith when we speak the Word of God in our prayers!

God gives us more insight in the following verses:

> **For as the rain cometh down, and the snow from heaven, and returneth not thither, but watereth the earth, and maketh it bring forth and bud, that it may give seed to the sower, and bread to the eater:**
> **So shall my word be that goeth forth out of my mouth: it shall not return unto me void, but it shall accomplish that which I please, and it shall prosper in the thing whereto I sent it.**
> —ISAIAH 55:10-11

We must pay close attention to what God is saying in these Scriptures. The key word here is "return." He is telling us that His Word will not be void, empty or unproductive, if we send it back to Him. So now the question is, how do we do that? The answer is simple. We return His Word to Him *in prayer.* And in His infinite goodness, He put His Words in a book called the Bible, so that we would know exactly how He would have us to pray! And nowhere in His Word does it tell us to pray His Word in a language we don't know or cannot comprehend. It is the act of praying and declaring the Word of God that is the guaranteed way to get answers and results, because we have given the Holy Spirit something He can move on and bring to pass.

Jesus Himself said:

> **If ye abide in me, and my words abide in you, ye shall ask what ye will, and it shall be done unto you.**
> —JOHN 15:7

The Sword of the Spirit

And take the helmet of salvation, and the sword of the Spirit, which is the word of God:
Praying always with all prayer and supplication in the Spirit, and watching thereunto with all perseverance and supplication for all saints;
—EPHESIANS 6:17-18

If there is a verse in Scripture that demonstrates the power and importance of the Word of God in prayer, it is Ephesians 6:17-18. Here, the Word of God is called "**the sword of the Spirit**." The Sword of the Spirit is the only offensive weapon in the armor of God. To go into prayer without the Word of God, is to go without the Holy Spirit's weapon! "**Praying always with all prayer and supplication in the Spirit**" follows the command to take the "**sword of the Spirit, which is the word of God**". The instruction is that, in order to pray "**in the Spirit,**" we must take the Word of God! The colon behind verse 17 connects the statement that follows. Verse 17 says to "**take... the sword of the Spirit, which is the word of God:**" and verse 18 tells us where to take it! So, according to the Word of God, we are to take the sword of the Spirit, which is the Word of God, into prayer as we pray "**in the Spirit.**"

Jesus' Instruction on Prayer

If there's any example that we, as Christians, should follow, it should be that of Jesus, the Christ. In the Book of Matthew, Jesus taught his disciples how to pray, and not one time, did He instruct us to pray with an "unknown tongue" that we don't understand, or to seek a perfect "prayer language." He said,

After this manner therefore pray ye: Our Father which art in heaven, Hallowed be thy name.
Thy kingdom come. Thy will be done in earth, as it is in heaven.

Give us this day our daily bread.

And forgive us our debts, as we forgive our debtors.

And lead us not into temptation, but deliver us from evil: For thine is the power, and the glory, forever. Amen.

—MATTHEW 6:9-13

Jesus gives us an outline of how to pray. He was not necessarily saying that we should pray these exact words, but rather, pray "after this manner".

According to this outline, we should start off our prayer by addressing our heavenly Father. We then magnify His Name through worship and thanksgiving. The next step is to call on His Kingdom. Jesus said to **"seek first the kingdom"** in Matthew 6:33, and the Kingdom of God is **"righteousness, and peace, and joy in the Holy Ghost"** (Romans 14:17). The word *kingdom* is made up of two words, *king* and *domain* or *dominion*. When we call on the Kingdom, we are calling on the King's dominion to come into our life.

After we call on God's Kingdom, we are to pray for His will to be done on earth (in our lives), as it is in heaven. This is where our knowledge of the Word comes in. We read earlier how His Word gives us His thoughts and how it bears record in heaven. Therefore, we should not pray words like the following example: "Lord, if it be your will that I die in this sickness, let it be done." We have His Word, so we pray with confidence and full assurance in this manner: "Father, I thank You that Your Word declares that by the stripes of Jesus I am healed (Isaiah 53:5) and that You wish above all things that I prosper and be in health" (3 John 2). We pray in this manner because we know that His Word *is* His will!

And this is the confidence that we have in him, that, if we ask any thing according to his will, he heareth us.

—1 JOHN 5:14

Then we pray for provision, **"Give us this day our daily bread."** We are praying, "Father, I thank You that You have supplied all of my need according to Your riches in heaven" (Philippians 4:19).

Then we forgive others and ask for forgiveness. "Father, I thank You that I have forgiveness, for You said if I would confess my sins that You would be faithful and just to forgive me and cleanse me from all unrighteousness" (1 John 1:9). Then we began to worship and magnify God.

During our prayer - whether at the beginning, the middle, or at the closing - we must be sure to declare the Name of Jesus! "**And whatsoever ye shall ask in my name, that will I do, that the Father may be glorified in the Son. If ye shall ask any thing in my name, I will do it**" (John 14:13-14). We should always pray in the Name of Jesus!

It is *impossible* to both pray after the manner that Jesus has instructed, and pray in some ecstatic, unknown, barbarian-like utterance. I was preaching a revival once and before services I stepped into one of the classrooms to pray. Shortly after I began to declare the Word of God, a man stepped into the room and began to pray, supposedly 'in the spirit.' He began to speak the exact same sounds over and over again. It was extremely distracting, and I could hardly keep my focus on my communion with God. This man, and so many others would benefit by this often overlooked instruction regarding prayer that Jesus gave, "**But when ye pray, use not vain repetitions, as the heathen do: for they think that they shall be heard of their much speaking**" (Matthew 6:7). Jesus said, don't pray "vain" or empty, meaningless repetitions. Yet, many of us have heard these meaningless sounds spoken in a redundant manner in various assemblies, even though it is contrary to the instructions Jesus gave us. The one way we can be totally confident that we are praying the way He would have us, is to pray the Word of God. His Word is never in vain!

> **Therefore I say unto you, What things soever ye desire, when ye pray, believe that ye receive them, and ye shall have them.**
>
> —MARK 11:24

If we pray in an *unknown tongue*, how can we *have* what we've asked for, if we don't even know *what* we have asked? It's not possible. That's why we must recognize that the instructions which

Jesus gives us regarding prayer do not lead us to the ecstatic sounds that so many are taught to pray.

The Intercession of The Holy Spirit

Another verse of Scripture that is often used to explain and support the belief of praying in an ecstatic voice is found in the Book of Romans. Let's take a closer look:

Likewise the Spirit also helpeth our infirmities: for we know not what we should pray for as we ought: but the Spirit itself maketh intercession for us with groanings which cannot be uttered.
—ROMANS 8:26

This verse is truly self-explanatory. The Holy Spirit makes intercession for us with groanings that cannot be uttered. That word 'groanings' comes from a Greek word *'stenazo'* which means inaudible prayers. That is explained in the last words of this verse, **"which cannot be uttered."** The word 'uttered' is translated from its' original Greek word, *'alaletos',* which means unspeakable.

This verse would be false if we were able to hear or speak these 'groanings'. So, we know that this Scripture is not telling us that the intercessions of the Holy Spirit are indistinguishable sounds that we are supposed to make, because that would make the prayers 'uttered and audible.' It is a mistake to believe that the Holy Spirit needs our assistance in making these intercessions! But many have been taught to believe that this verse is saying that when we pray an ecstatic, unknown language, the Spirit is speaking words through our mouth that cannot be uttered in our native or learned tongue. That is not what this verse says. If that were so, then it would violate the very meaning of intercession. The word 'intercession' is defined as prayer or petition on the behalf of another. Can you imagine someone coming over to your house and engaging themselves in your prayer and saying "Pray this, pray that and pray this," and then thanking you for interceding for them? Of course not! That would not be intercession. Intercession is when we pray for another as an act of our own will. We can pray for ourselves, but we cannot make the Holy Spirit, or anyone else, intercede for us! That would no longer be *intercession*, by definition of the word

Romans 8:26 is speaking of a prayer of intercession made by the Spirit alone. It doesn't say "the Spirit, with our help." It says "**the Spirit itself**." The Holy Spirit, alone, makes this intercession for us. He prays constantly on our behalf!

The Bible also teaches that Jesus, in total agreement with the Holy Spirit, intercedes for us.

> **Wherefore he is able also to save them to the uttermost that come unto God by him, seeing he ever liveth to make intercession for them.**
> —HEBREWS 7:25

Isn't that just like our God? He keeps His own commandments. If He tells us to intercede for each other, He's going to do it too!

We see in the following Scripture that God tells us to make intercession for others:

> **I exhort therefore, that, first of all, supplications, prayers, intercessions, and giving of thanks, be made for all men; For kings, and for all that are in authority; that we may lead a quiet and peaceable life in all godliness and honesty.**
> —1 TIMOTHY 2:1-2

There's an interesting point to be made in light of this topic. I had a woman, who was very bitter at God, approach me some years ago. She was upset because she had prayed over her loved one during a health emergency, and the individual died. She asked me why God allowed that to happen, considering that she prayed for hours "in the spirit," using her perfect "prayer language." I am not going to say that the outcome would have changed had this woman prayed differently. That's not my point in bringing up this particular situation. What I am trying to get across is that we can not Biblically intercede for someone using this unknown "prayer language," when we don't even know what we are saying.

A friend of mine approached me recently and asked me about a co-worker's prayers for him. He informed me that his co-worker told him that he had prayed for him using his *unknown prayer language*. What did he pray? How could it be said that he prayed for someone when he didn't know what he was saying? And according to this *doctrine of prayer languages*, how can he know that he prayed for a *specific* person? This is not intercession! Furthermore, if he didn't know what he was saying in his *"prayer language,"* how would he know when or if his prayer was answered?

The Word teaches us in James 5:15 that **"the prayer of faith shall save the sick, and the Lord shall raise him up; and if he have committed sins, they shall be forgiven him."** Remember that Romans 10:17 says that faith comes by hearing the Word of God. A prayer of faith is a prayer that is based on the Word of God. The Bible clearly tells us that if we pray the Word, we can go before God in thanks, and say, as the Psalmist said, **"Thou hast dealt well with thy servant, O LORD, according unto thy word"** (Psalms 119:65). In contrast, how can I say whether or not the Lord answered a specific prayer if I did not know what I was praying in this *"unknown prayer language?"*

Jesus' Testimony of the Holy Spirit

Jesus informed His disciples of the coming of the Holy Spirit. He used such titles as 'Comforter' and the 'Spirit of Truth.' He taught us what the Holy Spirit's role would be in our lives. Notice the following verses:

But when the Comforter is come, whom I will send unto you from the Father, even the Spirit of truth, which proceedeth from the Father, he shall testify of me:
And ye also shall bear witness, because ye have been with me from the beginning.
—JOHN 15:26-27

Jesus spoke of how He would send the Holy Spirit and what the Spirit's ministry on the earth would be. To be sure that the disciples knew what to expect, Jesus stated that they would be able to bear witness with the Holy Spirit because they had been with Him (Jesus) from the beginning. In other words, they would recognize the Holy Spirit because He would share the same attributes as Christ Himself. He goes on to give them an exact outline of what the Holy Spirit would do:

Nevertheless I tell you the truth; It is expedient for you that I go away: for if I go not away, the Comforter will not come unto you; but if I depart, I will send him unto you.

And when he is come, he will reprove the world of sin, and of righteousness, and of judgment:

Of sin, because they believe not on me;

Of righteousness, because I go to my Father, and ye see me no more;

Of judgment, because the prince of this world is judged.

I have yet many things to say unto you, but ye cannot bear them now.

Howbeit when he, the Spirit of truth, is come, he will guide you into all truth: for he shall not speak of himself; but whatsoever he shall hear, that shall he speak: and he will shew you things to come.

He shall glorify me: for he shall receive of mine, and shall shew it unto you.

—JOHN 16:7-15

Verse 8 in this text is a basic thesis statement. It gives the three points that Jesus listed as the role of the Holy Spirit. **"And when he is come, he will reprove the world of sin, and of righteousness, and of judgment."** In verses 9-11, He elaborates on these three points.

Now let's look at what Jesus said in reference to the Holy Spirit's ministry in verses 14-15. First, He said that the Spirit of Truth would guide us "**into all truth**." John 17:17 teaches us that the Word of God is Truth. So the ministry of the Holy Spirit would be to lead us in the Word. Secondly, He said that the Holy Spirit would not speak of Himself, but rather what He hears—from God the Father—would He speak to us. He would also show us things to come, which is prophecy. And finally, Jesus concluded his teaching by saying that the Holy Spirit would glorify Him.

After reading this list from Jesus Himself, one would have to wonder, in all that Jesus said about the coming of the Holy Spirit - His ministry, His purpose, His attributes and His power – why didn't Jesus ever say *anything* about the Holy Spirit imparting unto us a prayer language? If it was needful, isn't it something Jesus would have mentioned specifically? This would, hypothetically, have been the proper time to tell us, "And when the Spirit of Truth is come He will give you a perfect prayer language that you will not be able to understand," wouldn't it? In all seriousness, it's foolish to believe that Jesus would have omitted telling us about something as important and vital as a perfect *"prayer language."* Or could it be that He never mentioned it because no such language exists? Jesus made prayer simple when He said, **"If ye shall ask any thing in my name, I will do it"** (John 14:14).

Chapter 5

HOW DO WE LEARN TO DISCERN SPIRITS?

<u>Hate Every False Way</u>

It is *vital* that we, as believers, know how to discern the spirits. In this chapter, we will discover a sure way of distinguishing between what is of God and what is not. Before we can ever detect what is evil, or not of God, we first must be able to recognize the truth that which *is* of God.

One definite way of determining whether a spirit or individual is of God is by using the Word of God. Jesus said, **"He that is of God heareth God's words: ye therefore hear them not, because ye are not of God"** (John 8:47). It is impossible for someone to say that he or she is a believer, yet not have an appetite and desire for the Word of God. His Word is a discerner, and by using it, we also learn discern what is good and what is evil.

> **For every one that useth milk is unskillful in the word of righteousness: for he is a babe.**
>
> **But strong meat belongeth to them that are of full age, even those who by reason of use have their senses exercised to discern both good and evil.**
> **—HEBREWS 5:13-14**

This verse reiterates that it is by our using and becoming skillful in the Word of God that we train our senses to recognize the difference between good and evil. It is impossible to have discernment without being skillful in the Word of God. For this very reason, I have used over <u>150</u> Scripture references, throughout this book, to give clear understanding of the topics. When you have finished reading, your senses will be able to discern between truth and error, by the Word of God!

Therefore I esteem all thy precepts concerning all things to be right; and I hate every false way.
—PSALMS 119:128

The Psalmist is saying that he trusts that the Word of God is right about all things, and that he hates every way that is not according to the precepts, or the Word of God. When we look into the truth of God's Word, we have to make the decision to believe it and to live by it—even if it goes against our traditions or opinions:

Making the word of God of none effect through your tradition, which ye have delivered: and many such things do ye.
—MARK 7:13

Sadly, I have seen this Scripture come to pass, time after time. I have ministered the Word of God to an individual, and they would not receive it because it wasn't what they had been taught, or it didn't agree with their opinion. We must lay aside our tradition! We have to stop living our lives under the influence of other people, and receive the Word of God as infallible Truth! The more truth we gain an understanding of, the less likely it is that we will be subject to being deceived. I often tell my members at Word of God Ministries, "As much truth as I give you from the Word of God, you should never be deceived!" And truly we can stand on that because truth truly is the enemy to deception and error!

Believe Not Every Spirit

Beloved, believe not every spirit, but try the spirits whether they are of God: because many false prophets are gone out into the world.

— 1 JOHN 4:1

"**Howbeit when he, the Spirit of Truth, is come, he will guide you into all truth: for he shall not speak of himself; but whatsoever he shall hear, that shall he speak: and he will shew you things to come**" (John 16:13).There are two major points that we can learn about the Holy Spirit through this verse. The first is that He is a Spirit of Truth. John 17:17 says, "**thy word is truth.**" Therefore, we could make a substitution and say that the Holy Spirit is a Spirit *of the Word*. That means that all He says and does will come out of the Word, or will be done by the Word. This is His purpose—to lead us into truth, which is the Word of God. So we know, from this Scripture, that whenever the Holy Spirit is at work, the result will align with and be in accordance with the Word of God. If we witness any 'spiritual' manifestations that do not agree with the Word of God, we know that it is not by the Holy Spirit, because He only operates in line with truth!

The second thing we learn is, "**he shall not speak of himself.**" The Holy Spirit came not to be glorified, but to glorify Jesus. "**He shall glorify me: for he shall receive of mine, and shall shew it unto you**" (John 16:14). This will always be the case! The Holy Spirit is not a selfish showman, and if He moves, it is in line with the Word and for the glory of Jesus Christ.

I can recall being in a meeting some years ago; the preacher came to the platform and as he began his prayer, before thousands of people, he started laughing. He then said, "Come on now Holy Spirit, I am trying to pray." Supposedly, the Holy Spirit had interrupted his prayer with some type of spirit of laughter. Shortly thereafter, the whole congregation was falling over, laughing and out of control. Throughout this lengthy service, the Word of God was never opened and no one heard the Gospel of Jesus, the Anointed One. How did anyone receive faith if they did not hear God's Word

(Romans 10:17)? But supposedly, they had experienced a great move of the Spirit of God. Yet the Spirit of God moves only by the Word of God! This scenario goes completely against everything the Bible has told us of the Holy Spirit and His ministry. This is a clear example of why we were told, **"Beloved, believe not every spirit"** (1 John 4:1)!

In every occasion recorded in God's Word where the power of the Spirit was present, we also see the preaching of the Word of God. The Bible says, in Luke 4:14, that Jesus was in the power of the Spirit, and He taught in their synagogues. Notice what was said of Him: **"And they were astonished at his doctrine: for his word was with power"** (Luke 4:32). **"And they were all amazed, and spake among themselves, saying, What a word is this! For with authority and power he commanded the unclean spirits, and they come out"** (Luke 4:36). It was the power of His Word that drew the lost and drove out the devils!

> **But when the Comforter is come, whom I will send unto you from the Father, even the Spirit of Truth, which proceedeth from the Father, he shall testify of me:**
>
> **And ye also shall bear witness, because ye have been with me from the beginning.**
> —JOHN 15:26-27

The Spirit of Truth will *always* testify of Jesus. Jesus told his disciples that they would know the Spirit of Truth because of the relationship they had with Him. It is by our relationship with Jesus, the Word of God, that we bear witness with the Spirit of Truth. Whenever someone asks me if something was by the Spirit of God, I reply, "Would Jesus do that?" For example, a woman once visited a church service, and the minister poured a pitcher of water on her head. He said that it was a sign of the spirit. She later came and shared the experience with me, concerned about the matter, and wanted to know the truth. I asked her, "Would Jesus pour water on you and mess up your nice dress, so that you had to sit through the remainder of the service wet?" When she replied, "No," I said, "Then there's your answer." On another occasion, I was in a meeting in Houston, Texas, where a lady was out of control. Several men formed a circle around her to protect her, because she had been running into walls. This was supposedly by the Spirit, but my question was, "Would Jesus have done that to that lady?" Never! And the answer to that question will always show us if something is by the operation of the Holy Spirit or not. Therefore we should be able to identify the true works of Spirit of Truth through our relationship with Jesus.

The Spirits of the Prophets Are Subject to the Prophets

"And the spirits of the prophets are subject to the prophets" (1 Corinthians 14:32). Before we believe stories about how the Spirit of God drove someone out of control, we should examine the Word of God. According to this Scripture, no one can blame the Holy Spirit if he or she lost all control. Either the choice was made to lose control, or there was another spirit that took over.

The Spirit of God is a gentle spirit that leads His people. The Spirit of God never drives – it's not His nature. But it *is* the nature of the enemy. There are no occasions in the Book of Acts (The Actions of the Apostles) where the Spirit of God came on someone and they lost control. But the Bible illustrates many occasions where the Spirit of God manifested, and the Word of God was preached – the message of Jesus and the burden-removing, yoke-destroying power of God.

There was a man recorded in the Gospel of Luke that was demon-possessed and out-of-control. Jesus saved this man and the Bible says that man was seen **"sitting at the feet of Jesus, clothed, and in his right mind"** (Luke 8:35). Notice also what the Scripture says in Isaiah 1:18: **"Come now, and let us reason together, saith the Lord."** You can't reason if you are out-of-control!

So many have blamed the Holy Spirit for strange events where they were driven out-of-control. Galatians 5:22-23 says that one of the fruits of the Spirit is temperance, which means self-control. Jesus said that we would know them by their fruits (Matthew 7:16, 20; John 15). So we must ask ourselves, how could the Holy Spirit drive a person out of control, when one of His fruits, or productions, is self-control? We need to stop lying on God, and start taking responsibility for our actions! Many preachers are more worried about their prayer candidate falling over when hands are laid on them when, instead, they should be concerned if this person really knows Jesus. I've seen prayer lines where hands were laid and the candidate fell over while watching to see who was going to catch them. That could not have been a sincere reaction. But it's time for men and women of God to be real. I am not saying that I don't believe in God's manifestations. I am saying that we need to let God be God, and let us be ministers. When there are churches who have ushers trained to tug the shoulders of those who are receiving prayer, and the minister pushes their heads back in order to instigate a fall, that's disingenuous! We see many instances of those who had fallen out at the presence of God in Scripture. In some cases the men fell to their knees, or prostrate before Him. But nowhere in the Word does it say that an individual must fall back as a manifestation of God's touch. And I have never read one instance in Scripture where there was someone instructed to catch the one who fell under God's power. We need to check our hearts, determine our motives and allow the Word of God to teach us to discern spirits:

And he said unto them, Ye are they which justify yourselves before men; but God knoweth your hearts: for that which is highly esteemed among men is abomination in the sight of God.
—LUKE 16:15

Seducing Spirits

Before anyone welcomes the teaching that says God would have us speak to Him in a language that is unintelligible, there are some things that person should take into consideration. Let's see the testimony of Max Debono-DeLaurentis, who is a former Satanist:

"When I was heavily involved in the occult/new age, one of the most important forms of developing your communion with the spirits was through mantra chanting and emptying the mind to hear what the spirit has to say to you. I understood that I was to hear my spirit tell me what to do. It worked, and I have the emotional scars to prove it. When I got saved and set free through the shed Blood of Jesus and His resurrection, I believed this stuff was all behind me. I had repented of the occult practices I was involved in, from Martial Arts to Satan worship. In the last 20 years as a believer I have seen more and more practices I thought I had left behind coming into the church and believers calling it Christian and Biblical. These practices have been around for three thousand years or so, and never until recently have they been called Biblical."
[source: www.maxddl.org/Contemplative Prayer.htm]

So we see, through a firsthand testimony, that incomprehensible utterances are not used only among believers. 'Tongue' speaking and mantras are reported among Christians, the heathen, possessed people, tribal dancers, witch doctors and spiritual mediums, such as psychics and fortune-tellers. How can it be that Christians have something in common with these devilish groups? What has the Light to do with such darkness?

The following is a quote taken from an article of Hinduism: The Power of Mantra Chanting, *Why and How to Chant* by Gyan Rajhans.

"That which uplifts by constant repetition is a Mantra... The sacred utterances or chanting of Sanskrit Mantras provide us with the power to attain our goals and lift ourselves from the ordinary to the higher level of consciousness. They give us the power to cure diseases; ward off evils; gain wealth; acquire supernatural powers; worship a deity for exalted communion and for attaining blissful state and attain liberation."

Let me show an example of a Yoga Chant with a Sanskrit language and the English translation:

SANSKRIT
Om Om Om
Om Thryambakam Yajaamahe
Sugandhim Pushti-Vardhanam
Urvaarukamiva Bandhanaan
Mruthyor Muksheeya Maamruthath.

Om Namah Sivaaya Gurave
Satchidaananda Moorthaye
Nish Prapanjaaya Shaanthaaya
Niraalambaaya Thejase.

ENGLISH
We worship the three-eyed One who is fragrant and who nourishes all beings.
May he liberate us from death for the sake of Immortality,
Even as the cucumber is severed from its bondage of the creeper.

Om! Salutation to the Guru
who is Siva (auspiciousness),
who is the embodiment of Existence/ Knowledge/Bliss,
who is free from world consciousness,
who is peaceful, without support and
Self-effulgent.

I have no doubt that someone could walk in certain churches and began to chant the sounds I've quoted above that were taken from Yoga; likewise, there would be those in the church who would call it *tongues*, because the distinction between the ministry of the Holy Ghost and demonic spiritual activity has been so marred by the incorrectly taught traditions of men! Again, that's why the Word of God says, **"But if there be no interpreter, <u>let him keep silence in the church</u>; and let him speak to himself, and to God"** (1 Corinthians

14:28, emphasis mine); otherwise, anything would be allowed in the general assembly of the church, and there would be no one around to show the error of what was being said and done. And it is disturbing, in light of what we are reading, to know that the Holy Spirit is still being called the author of such blatant error and confusion!

> **Now the Spirit speaketh expressly, that in the latter times some shall depart from the faith, giving heed to seducing spirits, and doctrines of devils.**
> **—1 TIMOTHY 4:1**

I am not at all insinuating that Christians *knowingly* are taking part in a practice that is commonly used by those in the occult. I am saying that we need to examine the Word of God, before we open up our lives to demonic influence and seducing spirits.

> **Wherefore I give you to understand, that no man speaking by the Spirit of God calleth Jesus accursed: and that no man can say that Jesus is the Lord but by the Holy Ghost.**
> **—1 CORINTHIANS 12:3**

When someone speaks in an unknown tongue, it is uncertain what is being said, so unless someone who speaks that particular language—an interpreter—is present to explain what was spoken, anything, good or bad, could be declared, and the congregation would be none the wiser. In reference to the Scripture quoted above, how do we know if someone is not calling "Jesus accursed" in another *tongue* within our midst?

Familiar Spirits

Even though the most common teachings come from Acts and Corinthians, it is a mistake to believe that ecstatic sounds or 'tongues' were first spoken in the New Testament.

And when they shall say unto you, Seek unto them that have familiar spirits, and unto wizards that peep, and that mutter: should not a people seek unto their God? For the living to the dead?

To the law and to the testimony: if they speak not according to this word, it is because there is no light in them.

$\qquad$ —ISAIAH 8:19-20

In the Old Testament, God's people were given false counsel to seek those who were under the influence of a familiar spirit (interpreted as a 'happy' or 'emotional spirit'). These people were acting as spiritual mediums. Supposedly, they were speaking to God on behalf of man in an ecstatic utterance. God asks His people, **"why do you seek the living among the dead?"** He instructs them to seek the law and the testimony, which is his Word. The Bible says that those under the influence of this emotional, happy spirit would **"peep and mutter."**

These words are translated in their original Hebrew language to mean 'chatter,' which is the Hebrew word *'tsaphaph'*. It is defined as 'to utter speech-like but meaningless sounds: to talk idly, incessantly, or fast: to speak repeatedly or uncontrollably – chatter.'

And thou shalt be brought down, and shalt speak out of the ground, and thy speech shall be low out of the dust, and thy voice shall be, as of one that hath a familiar spirit, out of the ground, and thy speech shall whisper out of the dust.

$\qquad$ —ISAIAH 29:4

There were no ecstatic languages on the day of Pentecost, nor were there interpreters, but the Bible says that everyone understood in his own tongue. All cases of ecstatic languages that are documented in history and the Word of God are linked to those of idolaters. God says, in Isaiah 59:3, that, when such language is used, that person's tongue has muttered (chattered) perverseness.

We've seen it proven, over and over, that when God's spirit comes upon His people, His Word will be in their mouth. **"As for me, this is my covenant with them, saith the Lord; My spirit that is upon thee, and my words which I have put in thy mouth, shall not depart out of thy mouth, nor out of the mouth of thy seed, nor out of the mouth of thy seed's seed, saith the Lord, from henceforth and for ever"** (Isaiah 59:21). That is how we know when the Spirit of God is in operation, and when there is some other spirit at work.

The Wisdom of God

Get wisdom, get understanding: forget it not; neither decline from the words of my mouth.
Forsake her not, and she shall preserve thee: love her and she shall keep thee.
Wisdom is the principle thing; therefore get wisdom: and with all thy getting get understanding.
—PROVERBS 4:5-7

In all that is of God - His Word, His Gifts, His Callings, Prayer, His Spirit and His Will - Wisdom is the principle thing. There is nothing that is of God that does not contain Wisdom. This verse declares that Wisdom is the "principle" thing. That word 'principle' is defined as, essential: the necessary thing, the most important thing - imperative. Just as flour is the principle ingredient to cake, Wisdom is the essential ingredient to anything that is of God.

Though Wisdom can be defined many ways, the Scriptures define Wisdom to be the Word of God. **"Therefore also said the wisdom of God"** (Luke 11:49). Wisdom is what God says – the Word of God. With this understanding, I could translate Proverbs 4:5-7 to say,

Get the Word of God, get understanding: forget it not; neither decline from the words of my mouth. Forsake not the Word of God, and the Word of God shall preserve

thee: love the Word of God and the Word of God shall keep thee. The Word of God is the principle thing; therefore get the Word of God: and with all thy getting get understanding!

With all of our getting from God's Word, we must be sure to get understanding! Notice His wording: "**with all thy getting get understanding.**" God wants us to get understanding in everything. There is nothing that God will require of us that neglects wisdom and understanding. We never have to accept counsel or instruction that doesn't line up with Wisdom or the Word of God, or leaves us void of understanding:

For God is not the author of confusion, but of peace, as in all churches of the saints.
—1 CORINTHIANS 14:33

There are distinct attributes that describe the Wisdom of God. Remember, if it lacks the Wisdom of God it is not of God. With that in mind, look at the following verse:

But the wisdom that is from above is first pure, then peaceable, gentle, and easy to be intreated, full of mercy and good fruits, without partiality, and without hypocrisy.
—JAMES 3:17

The first thing we see is how the Bible describes the Wisdom that is from above. That is important, when we consider how we read earlier that those who were under the influence of familiar spirits spoke out of the ground (Isaiah 29:4). Secondly, we read that the Wisdom of God is pure. It has no additives or impurities. It is gentle and easy to be accepted – this is very important to remember! Many false teachings are hard to understand, and even harder to accept as practice, so we should quickly recognize them as not coming from the Wisdom of God. The Wisdom of God is also full of mercy and good fruits. This means that its productions are always good! We read that in Proverbs 4. Wisdom offers many blessings. God's

Wisdom is without partiality, which simply means that He doesn't favor one with it, and not another, and it will work the same for everyone. Finally, the Wisdom of God is without hypocrisy – that means that it can't be faked. Either we have Wisdom, or we don't.

Here's what the Bible say's about how to receive wisdom. "**If any of you lack wisdom, let him ask of God, that giveth to all men liberally, and upbraideth not; and it shall be given him. But let him ask in faith, nothing wavering**" (James 1:5-6). This verse tells us that we can ask God for wisdom, but we must ask Him in faith. Remember, faith comes by hearing the Word of God (Romans 10:17). Therefore, we should ask God for Wisdom, as we position ourselves to hear His Word. We can't be wavering! We have to make the decision to tune out everything that is not His Word– including our tradition. Then, as we seek His Word, we should declare "Father, I ask you for Wisdom and I thank you that, because I am in your Word, I receive the Wisdom that I ask for, in Jesus' name. Amen."

There are many that put on pretenses when it comes to spiritual things. But two things are for certain—we can not fool God, and we can not fool our enemy. The Bible says in Acts 6 that Stephen was full of faith and the Holy Ghost (v.5). "**And they were not able to resist the wisdom and the spirit by which he spake**" (Acts 6:10). Jesus said, "**For I will give you a mouth and wisdom, which all your adversaries shall not be able to gainsay nor resist**" (Luke 21:15). When we are truly ready to put the enemies to our faith on the run – we will commit our life to the Wisdom of God, and with all our getting, get understanding!

Signs without Salvation

There is a serious epidemic of sign-seekers in the average church today. When we place more emphasis on witnessing signs, than we do on a person's reception of salvation, there's a serious problem in our midst. I received an email from a person who left church, convinced that she was not saved, because her pastor said that if she were truly saved, she would speak in tongues. Signs have become so sought-after in the Christian faith that some now believe that a person is lost if he or she has not experienced them! Is this Scriptural? Notice what Jesus said about those who trusted in their signs:

> **Not every one that saith unto me, Lord, Lord, shall enter into the kingdom of heaven; but he that doeth the will of my Father which is in heaven.**
>
> **Many will say to me in that day, Lord, Lord, have we not prophesied in thy name? And in thy name have cast out devils? And in thy name done many wonderful works?**
>
> **And then will I profess unto them, I never knew you: depart from me: ye that work iniquity.**
>
> —MATTHEW 7:21-23

This was an example of people who had the signs, but had no salvation. There is a serious danger in trusting in signs as proof of salvation. Even the Pharisees had cast out devils (Matthew 12:27), and they did not trust nor believe in Jesus as the Son of God and Savior of the world. Jesus said to those who trusted in their signs or works as evidence of their salvation, **"I never knew you,"** and He called their work iniquity. Jesus makes it clear that a person can only be saved by doing the will of God. What is the will of God for salvation? 1 Timothy 2:3-4 says, **"For this is good and acceptable in the sight of God our Saviour; who will have all men to be saved, and to come unto the knowledge of the truth."** So, we see from this Scripture that it is God's will for all men to be saved. And according to the Word of God, we are saved by faith.

> **That if thou shalt confess with thy mouth the Lord Jesus, and shalt believe in thine heart that God hath raised him from the dead, thou shalt be saved.**
>
> **For whosover shall call upon the name of the Lord shall be saved.**
>
> —ROMANS 10:9, 13

Salvation comes by total trust in Jesus - relying solely on His sinless life, His death, burial and resurrection. Ephesians 2:8-9 declares, "**For by grace are ye saved through faith; and that not of yourselves: it is the gift of God: Not of works, lest any man should boast.**"

God says here that salvation is not our work – it's not of ourselves, and not of works, or else we could boast in our works, just as those who we read of in Matthew 7 did. Salvation is by faith in Jesus alone. Romans 5:10 says that we are saved by *His* life – not ours!

God gives us many warnings throughout the Bible not to be deceived by, nor to trust in signs. Jesus said in Matthew 12:39 and in 16:4, "**An evil and adulterous generation seeketh after a sign; and there shall no sign be given to it, but the sign of Jonah.**" The only sign we need to prove our salvation is that Jesus died and on the third day (the sign of Jonah), He rose from the dead! Notice Mark 8:12, "**And he sighed deeply in his spirit, and saith, Why doth this generation seek after a sign?**"

Tongues were used as a sign to the Jews (as we studied earlier). The Bible says,

> **For the Jews require a sign, and the Greeks seek after wisdom,**
> **But we preach Christ crucified, unto the Jews a stumbling block, and unto the Greeks foolishness;**
> **But unto them which are called, both Jews and Greeks, Christ the power of God, and the wisdom of God.**
> — 1 CORINTHIANS 1:22-24

But to those of us who have accepted Christ, He has become our power and wisdom! Therefore we should seek, and trust, solely in Him, and not in signs.

Ministers of Satan

Before we conclude this study, I want you, the reader, to recognize, by the Word of God, that Satan himself has his own ministers who have been sent to deceive. This is why it's so important not to seek signs. **"For such are false apostles, deceitful workers, transforming themselves into the apostles of Christ. And no marvel; for Satan himself is transformed into an angel of light. Therefore it is no great thing if his ministers also be transformed as the ministers of righteousness; whose end shall be according to their works"** (2 Corinthians 11:13-15).

The first recorded words of the devil in the Bible are, **"Yea, hath God said...?"** (Genesis 3:1). The oldest strategy of the enemy, according to the Bible, is to use his craftiness to cause man to doubt, or question, what God's Word says, because then he can deceive him into believing that anything he can think of or concoct for his life is acceptable, and that there is no absolute Truth or standard of living. Is it any wonder that God would close out His Word with a warning not to take away from what His Word says, and not to add anything to what His Word says (Revelation 22:18-19)? Satan's main objective is to pervert the Word of God. So we must guard our hearts, and *never* allow our faith or convictions to be established on anything that is not rooted and founded in God's Word!

Conclusion

It is and has been my objective, through this teaching, to share the Word of God with simplicity and with understanding. It is not my desire to judge or condemn, but to share the Word of Truth. I believe that God's Word is filled with all the answers and solutions to man's needs - mentally, spiritually and physically. God says in Hosea 4:6, **"My people are destroyed for lack of knowledge"** and in Isaiah 5:13, He says, **"My people are gone into captivity because they have no knowledge."** I don't take for granted my calling as a Pastor. I know that I have a great responsibility to God first and then His people. **"And I will give you pastors according to my heart, which shall feed you with knowledge and understanding"** (Jeremiah 3:15). My calling is not to please men, to side with the crowd or to defend tradition. My calling is to feed God's people with knowledge and understanding of His Word. It is my sincere desire that through this book, you have been drawn closer to the Word of God. I pray that this study has answered questions, settled your mind and given you knowledge on this highly misunderstood topic. I pray that you walk away from this book with a clear understanding of God's Word on Tongues.

About the Author

James A. McMenis is pastor of Word of God Ministries in Shreveport, Louisiana. He began the ministry as a weekly Bible study at the age of 22 in September 1994. Since that time, the work has become a national out-reach. Through television, radio, Bible conferences, crusades and the local assembly, Pastor McMenis, Word of God Ministries and its Word Partners are carrying out the vision of "Ministering the Word." Pastor McMenis has dedicated his life to winning the lost to Jesus and making disciples of the saved (John 8:30-32). Through the anointing of wisdom, knowledge and understanding, Pastor McMenis expounds on the Word of God bringing clarity and making God's Word applicable to the hearer. The core conviction of his message is *"Preaching Jesus as the Manifested Word of God!"*

He and his wife Chrissy, have three children, James Christian, Jaron Michael and Lana Grace.